Letter to the Reader

AN EFFECTIVE TEXTBOOK IN ABNORMAL PSYCHOLOGY BRINGS CLINICAL MATERIAL, RESEARCH, AND TRENDS TO life so that readers may understand the current state of the field, appreciate its questions and dilemmas, and become excited about its growing body of knowledge. At the same time, there is no substitute for in-depth readings of clinical material and research investigations. With such readings, the field truly comes to life and the reader can fully appreciate the human issues, dilemmas, progress, and limitations of the field.

Thus, I am delighted to include with my textbooks, ABNORMAL PSYCHOLOGY and FUNDAMENTALS OF ABNORMAL PSYCHOLOGY, this collection of contemporary readings from the distinguished publication SCIENTIFIC AMERICAN. For years, the pages of SCIENTIFIC AMERICAN have offered readers a remarkably captivating look at current issues in science – from the natural to the social sciences. Its timely articles, presented by leading scientists and writers, have always been written in the spirit of an exciting detective novel – clarifying critical questions for readers, guiding them through a maze of relevant issues, and building to powerful conclusions.

This collection of SCIENTIFIC AMERICAN readings centers, of course, on topics in abnormal psychology. In the best tradition of the publication, readers will journey with the writers through an array of important clinical subjects, appreciating the logic behind relevant research, understanding where such work is leading, and finding themselves excited about what is going on. The articles in this collection include topics such as psychological wounds of war, women and depression, psychological disorders and creativity, hypertension in African-Americans, the placebo effect, false memories, and disorders like anorexia nervosa and attention-deficit hyperactivity disorder. So sit back, prepare to explore, and, most of all, enjoy the journey.

Ron Comer

Contents

KALAMAZOO VALLEY

COMMUNITY COLLEGE

A Gift to the KVCC Libraries from

J. STEPHEN NEYNABER

SCIENTIFIC AMERICAN
PSYCHOLOGY READER

to accompany:

Abnormal Psychology

Fundamentals of Abnormal Psychology

by Ronald J. Comer

INCLUDES:

Invisible Wounds
by Richard F. Mollica

Why Are So Many Women Depressed?
by Ellen Leibenluft

Manic-Depressive Illness and Creativity
by Kay Redfield Jamison

The Puzzle of Hypertension in African-Americans
by Richard S. Cooper et al.

The Placebo Effect
by Walter A. Brown

Dying to Be Thin
by Kristin Leutwyler

Creating False Memories
by Elizabeth F. Loftus

Attention-Deficit Hyperactivity Disorder
by Russell A. Barkley

Contents

Contents

Contents

Connecting with your customers is more than just good business...

it's a science.

Top marketers turn to
Scientific American Custom Media
to achieve their goals. Through highly relevant
and compelling content, Scientific American
captivates key decision-makers in medicine,
science, technology, business and public policy.

Whether you're positioning your brand as a thought
leader or generating leads, Scientific American
Custom Media will engage your audience with
targeted publications, special sections, websites,
podcasts, videos and events.

SCIENTIFIC
AMERICAN
CUSTOM
MEDIA

For more information contact:
Marc Richards @ 212.451.8859
mrichards@sciam.com

INVISIBLE WOUNDS

Medical researchers have recently begun to address the mental health effects of war on civilians

by Richard F. Mollica

The Khmer Rouge executed her entire family. Their beatings left her unconscious, lying on the bodies of her loved ones. When my first Cambodian patient told me this story in graphic detail in 1981, my initial reaction was that it simply couldn't be true. It seemed so unreal, like a scene taken straight from a horror movie. My instinct was to disbelieve.

My feeling was an example of what novelist Herman Wouk has called "the will not to believe." Such a response is a common reaction to accounts of human cruelty and emotional suffering, and it is one of the reasons that political leaders, humanitarian aid workers and even psychiatrists have failed to appreciate the depth of war's trauma. The model used to be a rubber band. War is hell, but we thought that once a conflict ended, those affected would snap back to normal. Physical injuries would linger, but the anxiety and fear that accompany any life-threatening event should disappear once the immediate danger passes. The general public had much the same attitude. In essence, the message from the outside world to war's victims was: Be tough. Just get over it.

Indeed, that was the thinking about most traumatic events, from child abuse to rape. Now we know better. Awful experiences can cause damage that does not always heal naturally; the victims may need counseling, economic assistance and medication. Post-traumatic stress disorder (PTSD) was officially recognized in 1980, partly because of the experience of U.S. veterans of the Korean and Vietnam wars. But it has only been in the past two decades that researchers have doc-

umented the social and emotional consequences of war for civilian populations. These findings are revolutionizing the recovery of societies devastated by war.

In 1988 our team at Harvard University, with the support of the World Federation for Mental Health, sent a psychiatric team to Site 2, the largest Cambodian refugee camp on the Thai-Cambodian border. We interviewed 993 camp residents, who recounted a total of 15,000 distinct trauma events, such as kidnapping, imprisonment, torture and rape. Yet the international authorities charged with protecting and providing for the camp had made no provisions whatsoever for mental health services. Similar lapses affected other refugee operations the world over. Over time the reason became clear: the mental health effects of mass violence are invisible.

Put simply, it is easier to count dead bodies and lost limbs than shattered minds. Wounded people readily seek out doctors, but the stigma of mental illness is high, so traumatized people typically avoid psychiatrists at all costs. The lack of standardized criteria for mental health disorders and the differences among cultures have also contributed to the neglect. Local folk diagnoses may not match the disease categories of Western medicine.

The survivors of mass violence often keep their feelings to themselves because they fear misunderstanding—with good reason. In his memoirs, Primo Levi describes the fantasies he had while at Auschwitz. He dreamed of seeing his family again but also dreaded it: "It is an intense pleasure, physical,

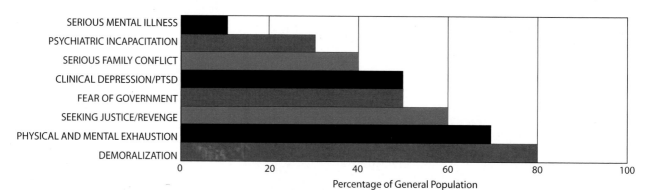

NEARLY EVERYBODY in a society at war is traumatized to some degree, ranging from serious mental illness (such as psychosis) to clinical depression and post-traumatic stress disorder. According to these composite statistics from recent civil wars, the vast majority of civilians are exhausted, despairing and mistrustful, which wrecks the social fabric for a generation or longer.

inexpressible to be at home, among friendly people and to have so many things to recount; but I cannot help noticing that my listeners do not follow me. In fact, they are completely indifferent; they speak confidently of other things as if I were not there. My sister looks at me, gets up and goes away without a word—the grief is unbearable."

People's disbelief and disinterest are unfortunately quite real. They reflect the problem we all have in comprehending evil. How can human beings perpetrate such acts? Lacking a simple answer—and wishing to avoid our own intimations of guilt—we change the subject.

When international agencies finally began to address mental health, they first sought simple solutions. Yet providing mental health care is even less straightforward than rebuilding

levels of acute clinical depression and PTSD of 68 and 37 percent, respectively. Roughly similar numbers have been found among Bhutanese refugees living in Nepal and among Bosnian refugees living in Croatia. By comparison, in nontraumatized communities rates of 10 percent for depression and 8 percent for PTSD (over a lifetime) would be considered high.

Second, researchers have determined that the nature of the trauma can be rigorously measured. Psychiatrists used to worry that probing a patient's traumatic experiences would be too emotionally disturbing. They also felt that patients would provide inaccurate accounts, at best exaggerated and at worst outright lies. But beginning in the early 1980s, a new movement emerged in medicine, associated with the activities of groups such as Amnesty International. Human-rights research-

DRAGOBIL, KOSOVO, OCTOBER 28, 1998: A group of ethnic Albanian women weep over the body of Ali Murat Pacarizi, a 20-year old Kosovo Liberation Army soldier killed while trying to defuse a Serbian booby trap.

roads or treating malaria. Nevertheless, researchers have made headway; six basic discoveries point the way.

The first is the sheer prevalence of major psychiatric disorders among civilian survivors of war. Advances in psychiatric epidemiology—random samples of representative populations, utilization of lay interviewers and development of standardized criteria for diagnosis, even across cultures—have at last yielded reliable numbers. Our study of Cambodian refugees revealed

ers developed a systematic method that combines various types of clinical examinations to verify the accuracy of reports.

For instance, our clinical service found that psychiatric patients from Indochina who had suffered horrific brutality were unable to describe their experiences in a standard open-ended psychiatric interview. Instead we tried a simple screening instrument known as the Hopkins Symptom Checklist, which has been widely used in general populations since the 1950s. The list takes about 15 minutes to fill out and asks such questions as whether the respondent feels low on energy, has difficulty falling asleep or thinks about committing suicide. When we gave patients an Indochinese version of the checklist, they were able to relate their emotional reactions with little distress.

Invisible Wounds

A Historical Perspective
The Human Cost of War
Modern warfare kills more civilians than soldiers

by Walter C. Clemens, Jr., and J. David Singer

O ne of the most influential military thinkers of all time, 19th-century Prussian strategist Carl von Clausewitz, asserted that war should be seen as just another tool used by political leaders—"the continuation of policy by other means." But very often the motives that lead to war are lost in the vast destruction it causes.

Drawing data from a variety of sources, we have tried to gauge the relative severity of the principal international conflicts of the past two centuries [*see chart below*]. World Wars I and II were by far the most devastating in history, both in terms of battle deaths—military personnel killed in combat—and total deaths, which include the soldiers who died from wounds, accidents or disease, as well as the civilians killed. These numbers require some interpretation. First, the death tolls are only rough estimates. Second, they do not fully convey a war's effect on a nation or region, which is better expressed in terms of deaths per capita, or its impact on the friends and families of those who perish.

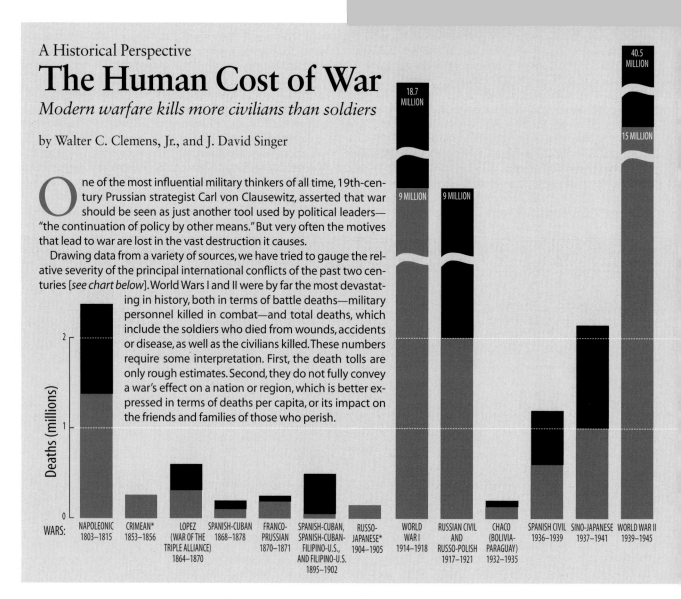

A modified checklist, the Harvard Trauma Questionnaire, focuses on trauma events and symptoms of PTSD. It now exists in more than 25 languages, tailored for each unique cultural context and tested empirically.

Using the Right Idiom

T hird, medical anthropologists have codified non-Western conceptions of mental health disorders. In many societies, traditional healers and community elders, rather than medical doctors, are the principal source of health care, particularly mental health care. But some patients fall through the cracks: traditional healers are not able to heal their condition, and doctors do not recognize their vague somatic complaints as symptoms of an underlying mental illness. Extensive fieldwork in Cambodia, Uganda and Zimbabwe has now catalogued the wide range of folk diagnoses associated with emotional suffering. Our team has produced an encyclopedia of these diagnoses for Cambodia, so that Western-oriented practitioners can identify mental illness using local idioms.

Fourth, particular traumatic experiences are more likely than others to lead to depression and PTSD. Among Cambodian refugees at Site 2, the most harmful incidents involved

blows to the head, other physical injury, incarceration, and watching the murder or starvation of a child. Lacking shelter and witnessing violence to other adults had less of an impact.

Fifth, some of the most potent events cause permanent organic changes in the brain. In the early 1960s, Norwegian researcher Leo Eitinger and his colleagues discovered a link between head injury and psychiatric symptoms in the survivors of Nazi concentration camps. According to more recent research, the beatings suffered by American POWs during World War II and the Korean and Vietnam wars often led to brain damage. Similarly, of 200 civilian torture survivors examined by Danish researcher Ole Rasmussen and his colleagues, 64 percent had neurological impairments. Even in the absence of direct physical injury, emotional distress can scar the brain. The few available studies of subjects with PTSD have revealed that certain structures in the brain, such as the hippocampus, shrink as a result of trauma. Some neuroscientists have begun to connect these early results to the persistent and debilitating symptoms of PTSD.

The sixth and final discovery demonstrates the connection between mental distress and social dysfunction. Last year my colleagues and I analyzed the serious disability associated with psychiatric distress among Bosnian refugees living in

From the end of the Thirty Years' War in 1648 to the French Revolution in 1789, Europe's princes fought one another with relatively small armies. France's upheavals, however, gave birth to the concept of a "nation in arms." Starting at the same time, the Industrial Revolution turned cities and factories into prime targets. In most wars of the past century, civilian deaths have outnumbered military deaths. Some countries have lost more than 10 percent of their population in a single war (for instance, the Soviet Union during World War II). Americans have been largely spared by geography.

Since World War II, Asia, Africa and the Middle East have become the world's primary battlegrounds. In the conflicts that raged in Angola and Mozambique from the 1960s to the 1990s, more than 75 percent of the victims were civilians. A large number were also children: between 1985 and 1995, some two million children died from warfare, and another 10 million to 15 million were maimed physically or psychologically. One reason for the high civilian death rate is that many of the international conflicts since 1945 began as civil wars. The Korean, Vietnamese and Afghan wars, among others, started as internal conflicts but soon attracted outside intervention.

Amid the "new world disorder" of the 1990s, war often became a private enterprise. In the conflicts that followed the breakup of Yugoslavia, for example, much of the fighting was conducted by bands of irregulars who served out of personal loyalty, hope for booty or lust for revenge. Meanwhile U.S. armed forces began to do less fighting and more peacekeeping. The U.S. and its allies were able to minimize their own casualties in the war with Iraq in 1991 and in the Kosovo operation last year. Whether they can do so in future conflicts, however, is uncertain. Even von Clausewitz acknowledged the risk of "friction" during warfare—his euphemism for all the things that can go horribly wrong.

WALTER C. CLEMENS, JR., and J. DAVID SINGER are professors of political science. Clemens teaches at Boston University and is also an associate at the Harvard University Belfer Center for Science and International Affairs. Singer teaches at the University of Michigan and also directs the Correlates of War Project.

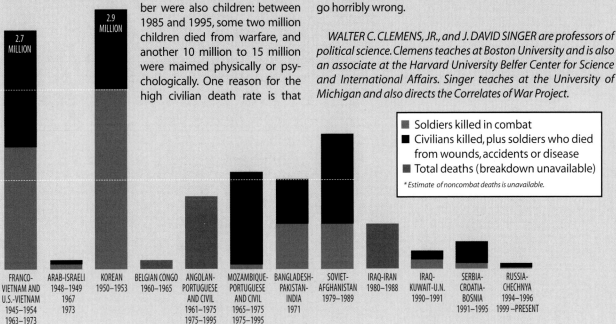

- ■ Soldiers killed in combat
- ■ Civilians killed, plus soldiers who died from wounds, accidents or disease
- ■ Total deaths (breakdown unavailable)

Estimate of noncombat deaths is unavailable.

2.7 MILLION — FRANCO-VIETNAM AND U.S.-VIETNAM 1945–1954 1963–1973

ARAB-ISRAELI 1948–1949 1967 1973

2.9 MILLION — KOREAN 1950–1953

BELGIAN CONGO 1960–1965

ANGOLAN-PORTUGUESE AND CIVIL 1961–1975 1975–1995

MOZAMBIQUE-PORTUGUESE AND CIVIL 1965–1975 1975–1995

BANGLADESH-PAKISTAN-INDIA 1971

SOVIET-AFGHANISTAN 1979–1989

IRAQ-IRAN 1980–1988

IRAQ-KUWAIT-U.N. 1990–1991

SERBIA-CROATIA-BOSNIA 1991–1995

RUSSIA-CHECHNYA 1994–1996 1999–PRESENT

Croatia. One in four were unable to work, care for their families or participate in other socially productive activities.

The long-term effects of such a mental health crisis are still unknown; few longitudinal studies have been done. A recent survey of a Dutch population found that people who had been targets of Nazi persecution had a higher rate of PTSD over the subsequent 50-year period. Such traumas may have multigenerational effects as well: researchers have noted higher rates of PTSD in the children of Holocaust survivors compared with a nontraumatized Jewish comparison group. But the relation of cause and effect remains unclear. Did the Nazi horrors directly cause the PTSD, did they leave survivors vulnerable to subsequent traumas, or is the correlation related to some other variable altogether? To understand the long-term consequences of war, we are now conducting a longitudinal study in Bosnia.

The bottom line is that although only a small percentage of survivors of mass violence suffer serious mental illness requiring acute psychiatric care, the vast majority experience low-grade but long-lasting mental health problems [*see illustration on page 2*]. For a society to recover effectively, this majority cannot be overlooked. Pervasive physical exhaustion, hatred and lack of trust can persist long after the war ends. Like chronic diseases such as malaria, mental illness can weigh down the economic development of a country.

Only within the past five years have international organizations recognized this fact. The World Bank, in particular, has acknowledged that old development models are not working for war-devastated nations and that new approaches are needed. International aid agencies have established community-based mental health clinics in Cambodia and East Timor, and local doctors in South Africa and Bosnia have appeared on television to publicize the problems and opportunities for care. Our own program is now setting up microenterprise projects to ease depressed people back into productive work. Such efforts are crucial to breaking the vicious cycle of lethargy and revenge that blights an ever greater area of the globe. ⬛

The Author

RICHARD F. MOLLICA is a professor of psychiatry at Harvard Medical School. In 1981 he co-founded the Harvard Program in Refugee Trauma, one of the first clinical centers in the U.S. for survivors of mass violence and torture. This article emerged from a course he taught earlier this year at Waseda University in Tokyo.

LAURIE GRACE

Why Are So Many D Women epressed?

Women may be more sensitive—physiologically, at least—to certain changes in the environment. And this responsiveness might help explain the high rates of depression in their ranks

by Ellen Leibenluft, M.D.
National Institute of Mental Health

The symptoms of depression range from uncomfortable to debilitating: sleep disturbances, hopelessness, feelings of worthlessness, difficulty concentrating, fatigue and sometimes even delusions. Most of us have watched a relative or friend struggle with depression—and many of us have experienced it ourselves. Even so,

few people realize just how common depression is, how severe it can be or that it is most prevalent among women. In 1990 the World Health Organization found depression to be the leading cause of "disease burden" (a composite measure including both illness and death) among women, noting that it affects almost 20 percent of the female population in the developed world. Epidemiological studies indicate that 12 percent of U.S. women—compared with only 6 percent of U.S. men—have suffered from clinically significant depression at some time in their lives.

The big question, of course, is why such a gender gap exists. Over the years various explanations have surfaced to account for the fact that, from one study to the next, depression is between two and three times more common among women than it is among men. Some mental health workers have pointed to psychology, arguing that women are better trained to recognize their feelings and seek help, so they come to the attention of health professionals more often than men. Others have suggested that oppression—in the form of physical or sexual abuse, harassment or discrimination—is to blame. Others still have attributed the increased rates of depression among women to the female reproductive system and the menstrual cycle.

But it isn't that simple. Data from a variety of

Medications known as selective serotonin reuptake inhibitors (SSRIs), which are often most effective when used in conjunction with psychotherapy, were approved for treating depression in the late 1980s. These drugs, which include Prozac, Paxil and Zoloft, act on the brain by regulating the neurotransmitter serotonin.

studies show that depression clearly has psychological, environmental and biological roots. Modern neuroscience is beginning to teach us how these roots can become intertwined and reinforce one another. In other words, an increased risk for depression in women might stem from genetics, the effects of stressful events or social pressures, or some combination of all three. Neuroimaging of the brain's circuitry by PET and MRI scans reveals that psychological phenomena such as anger and sadness have biological underpinnings; we can now see circuits of brain cells becoming activated when these emotions arise.

Similarly, neuroimages demonstrate that environmental and psychological experiences can alter our brain chemistry. For example, Lewis R. Baxter and his colleagues at the University of California at Los Angeles found similar changes on the PET scans of patients with obsessive-compulsive disorder who responded to treatment, regardless of whether the patients were treated with medication or with behavioral therapy.

To figure out why depression is more common among women, scientists have to study how genetics and environment divide the sexes—and how the two conspire to produce the symptoms we describe as depression. It is difficult work, and progress is necessarily slow. But what is coming into focus is that certain environmental factors—including stress, seasonal changes and social rank—may produce different physiological responses in females than they do in males. These findings, which I will outline, are small pieces in what is proving to be an incredibly complex puz-

Psychotherapy has long proved valuable in alleviating symptoms of depression. More than 80 percent of all depressed patients now respond to therapy or medication, or a combination of the two.

zle. Laying them out at this stage does not begin to explain depression's double standard. Nevertheless, it could help scientists develop more effective treatments for depressed individuals—both women and men—in the meantime.

Stress and Cortisol

Many scientists have wondered whether there is some quirk in the way depression is inherited, such that a depressed parent or grandparent is more likely to pass on a predisposition for the disorder to female than to male descendants. Based on studies that trace family histories of depression, the answer to that question appears to be no. Women and men with similar heritage seem equally likely to develop the disorder. Simply tracing family histories, though, without also considering environmental influences, might not offer a complete picture of how depression is inherited.

Indeed, Kenneth S. Kendler and his colleagues at the Medical College of Virginia found in a study of 2,060 female twins that genetics might contribute to how women respond to environmental pressures. The researchers examined twins with and without a family history of depression; some twins in both groups had recently undergone a trauma, such as the death of a loved one or a divorce. The investigators found that among the women who did not have a family history of depression, stressful events raised their risk for depression by only 6 percent. But the same risk rose almost 14 percent among the women who did have a family history of depression. In other words, these women had seemingly inherited the propensity to become depressed in the wake of crises.

A similar study has not been done in men, leaving open the question of whether environmental stress and genetic risk for depression interact similarly in both sexes. But research is being done to determine whether men and women generally experience similar amounts and types of stress. Studies of key hormones hint that they do not. Hormones are not new to depression researchers. Many have wondered whether the gonadal steroids estrogen and progesterone—whose cyclic fluctuations in wom-

en regulate menstruation—might put women at a greater risk for depression. There are at least two ways in which they might do so.

First, because of differences between the X and Y chromosomes, male and female brains are exposed to different hormonal milieus in utero. These hormonal differences may affect brain development so that men and women have different vulnerabilities—and different physiological reactions to environmental stressors—later in life. Indeed, animal experiments show that early hormonal influences have marked behavioral consequences later on, although the phenomenon is of course difficult to study in humans.

Second, the fact that postpubertal men and women have different levels of circulating gonadal steroids might somehow put women at higher risk for depression. Research shows girls become more susceptible to depression than boys only after puberty, when they begin menstruating and experience hormonal fluxes. Even so, scientists have never been able to establish a direct relation between emotional states and lev-

els of estrogen and progesterone in the blood of women. For example, Peter J. Schmidt and David R. Rubinow of the National Institute of Mental Health recently reported that manipulations of estrogen and progesterone did not affect mood, except in women who suffer from severe premenstrual mood changes.

It now appears, however, that estrogen might set the stage for depression indirectly by priming the body's stress response. During stressful times, the adrenal glands—which sit on top of the kidneys and are controlled by the pituitary gland in the brain—secrete higher levels of a hormone called cortisol, which increases the activity of the body's metabolic and immune systems, among others. In the normal course of events, stress increases cortisol secretion, but these elevated levels have a negative feedback effect on the pituitary, so that cortisol levels gradually return to normal.

Evidence is emerging that estrogen might not only increase cortisol secretion but also decrease cortisol's ability to shut down its own secretion. The result might be a stress response that is not only more pronounced but also

NAJLAH FEANNY SABA

longer-lasting in women than in men.

For example, Nicholas C. Vamvako-poulos, George P. Chrousos and their colleagues at the National Institute of Child Health and Human Development recently found that increased levels of estrogen heighten the activity of the gene for human corticotropin-releasing hormone (CRH). This gene controls the secretion of CRH by a region of the brain called the hypothalamus. CRH makes the pituitary gland release adrenocorti-cotropic hormone (ACTH), which circu-lates in the blood and eventually reach-es the adrenal glands, where it prompts the secretion of cortisol. Thus, estrogen can, by increasing CRH secretion, ulti-mately boost cortisol secretion. And Elizabeth A. Young of the University of Michigan and others have shown that female rats are more "resistant" to corti-sol's negative feedback effects than are either male rats or spayed female rats. She has also shown that women have long-er-lasting cortisol responses during the phase of the menstrual cycle when es-trogen and progesterone levels are high.

It is unclear whether depression is a cause or a consequence of elevated cor-tisol levels, but the two are undoubted-ly related. Over the past few decades, a number of studies have shown that cor-tisol levels are elevated in about half of all severely depressed people, both men and women. So the idea is this: if estro-gen raises cortisol levels after stress or decreases cortisol's ability to shut down its own secretion, then estrogen might render women more prone to depres-sion—particularly after a stressful event.

Light and Melatonin

Despite their importance, estrogen and cortisol are not the only hormones in-volved in female depression, and stress is not the only environmental influence that might hold more sway over women than men. Recent findings by Thomas A. Wehr, Norman E. Rosenthal and their colleagues at the National Institute of Mental Health indicate that women might be more responsive physiologi-cally than men to changes in exposure to light and dark. These investigators have had a long-standing interest in seasonal affective disorder (SAD), or so-called winter depression (although it can occur in the summer as well), and the role that the hormone melatonin might play in the illness. Similar to the gender ratio in other forms of depres-sion, SAD is three times more common in women than in men.

Melatonin has been a prime suspect in SAD because organisms (including hu-mans) secrete it only when they are in the dark and only when the body's in-ternal clock (located in the hypothala-mus) believes it is nighttime. The pineal gland, a small structure that resides deep in the mammalian brain, begins to se-crete melatonin in the evening, as day-light wanes. Melatonin levels drop in the morning, when light hits the retinas of the eyes. Because nights are longer in winter than in summer, animals living in the wild secrete melatonin for longer periods each day during winter. Among animals that breed in summer, the onset of this extended daily melatonin secre-tion signals the presence of winter and shuts down the secretion of gonadal steroids that facilitate reproduction.

SAD researchers have long wondered whether a wintertime increase in the dur-ation of melatonin secretion might also trigger depressive symptoms in suscepti-ble individuals. In a series of ongoing studies designed to address this ques-tion, Wehr and his colleagues first asked whether humans, like animals, undergo seasonal changes in melatonin secretion.

It is an important question, given that artificial light provides humans with an "endless summer" of sorts compared with animals in the wild. To find out, Wehr measured melatonin secretion in 15 humans when they were exposed to 14 hours of darkness and later to only eight hours of darkness each night. The results of this experiment, conducted mostly among men, were positive: peo-ple experiencing longer periods of dark-ness secreted melatonin for longer peri-ods during the night, as wild animals do.

Next, the researchers asked whether this natural sensitivity to the seasonal day-length change persisted when people were allowed to follow their usual sched-ules, turning on artificial lights at night as they normally would. Here the re-searchers were surprised to find a gender difference. Under normal living condi-tions, women were more likely than men to retain a sensitivity to seasonal changes in day length. In other words, for women the duration of nocturnal melatonin secretion was longer in win-ter than summer; in men, however, there was no seasonal difference.

These results suggest that women are more sensitive to natural light than men—and that in a society where arti-ficial light is everywhere, women some-how still detect seasonal changes in nat-ural day length. Whether this gender difference puts women at increased risk for SAD is unclear; paradoxically, there is evidence that women with SAD symp-toms may be less likely than unaffected women to have an increased duration of melatonin secretion in winter.

To complicate the story further, the relation between these findings and those regarding cortisol and estrogen are also unclear, because we don't know whether the duration of melatonin se-cretion affects reproductive function in women, as it surely does in animals. Re-searchers are now working to unravel the complicated relations between these hormonal systems and to determine whether, and how, they may influence individuals' risk for depression.

Social Rank and Serotonin

If women's bodies are in fact particularly sensitive to environmental changes, the explanation may lie within the system that controls serotonin, one of many so-called neurotransmitters that nerve cells use to communicate with one another. Serotonin modulates both cortisol and melatonin secretion. (The similarity in

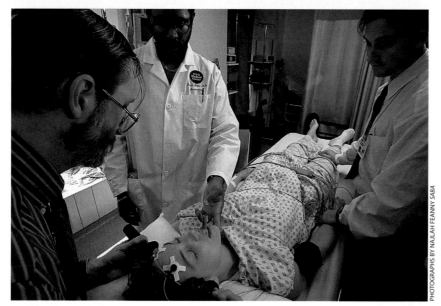

PHOTOGRAPHS BY NAJLAH FEANNY SABA

Treatment alternatives such as light therapy (top) and electroconvulsive therapy (ECT) (bottom) are used in special cases. Light therapy seems particularly effective in patients with the form of depression called seasonal affective disorder (SAD). ECT is most often used as a last resort, when all other treatment options have failed.

Mirko Diksic, Sadahiko Nishizawa and their colleagues at McGill University recently provided the most dramatic example: to measure serotonin synthesis in the human brain, they devised a new technique using PET neuroimaging and found that the average synthesis rate was 52 percent higher in men than in women. The investigators note that with the exception of estrogen binding sites, this gender difference in the brain is one of the largest ever reported. The lower rate of serotonin synthesis in women might increase their overall risk for depression—especially if serotonin stores are depleted during stress or winter darkness.

A Gender Difference

Meir Steiner and his co-workers at McMaster University suggest that if serotonin mediates between an organism and its environment and if the neurotransmitter is regulated differently in men and women, it might explain gender patterns not only in depression but also in a range of psychiatric illnesses. Specifically, whereas depression and anxiety are more common among women, alcoholism and severe aggression are more common among men. And just as low serotonin levels have been implicated in depression and anxiety disorders in women, they have also been found in the brains of men with severe forms of alcoholism and aggression.

Such gender differences in the serotonergic system might ensure that females respond to stress with psychiatric disturbances that involve behavioral inhibition, whereas men respond to stress with a loss of behavioral control. Steiner suggests that such gender differences in the serotonergic system evolved because child rearing is more successful (in the narrow sense of more children surviving to adulthood) in species in which aggressive impulses are curtailed in females.

A researcher espousing either the sociological or psychological explanation of depression's gender bias might counter Steiner's theory by arguing that men are socialized to respond to stress with "act-

names between serotonin and melatonin is no accident: the latter is synthesized directly from the former, and the two have very similar chemical structures.) And a great deal of evidence indicates that dysfunction in the serotonergic, or serotonin-secreting, system contributes to depression and anxiety disorders, which are also more common in women than men. Recently research in animals and humans has provided preliminary, but key, insights into this system.

First, it appears that the serotonergic system serves as a link between an animal's nervous system and its physical and social environment. That is, not only do stress and daylight act via the serotonergic system but an animal's social rank also appears to affect its serotonin

level. A number of studies show that blood and brain serotonin levels change as an animal moves up or down dominance hierarchies. For instance, dominant male monkeys often have higher blood serotonin levels than subordinate ones do. In addition, a recent study by Shih-Rung Yeh and his colleagues at Georgia State University shows that the sensitivity of an animal's neurons to serotonin varies according to that animal's status. Specifically, Yeh found that neurons taken from crayfish that had recently won a fight responded to serotonergic stimulation more strongly than neurons taken from losing crayfish.

There also appear to be significant gender differences in the serotonergic systems of both animals and humans.

Why Are So Many Women Depressed?

ing out" behaviors, such as alcoholism or aggression. In contrast, society teaches women to respond to stress with "acting in" behaviors, such as depression. To support this idea, they might point to epidemiological studies done in Amish and Jewish populations. In these communities, alcoholism is less common than in the population at large, and, interestingly, the rates of depression are as high in men as in women.

These contradictory data leave no doubt that the explanations behind depression and other psychiatric diseases are not straightforward. Biological and social influences not only coexist but also probably reinforce one another. After all, we would expect gender socialization patterns to evolve so that they complement biological differences between the sexes. In other words, we would expect "nurture" to reinforce rather than oppose "nature." And because nurture involves learning—and learning occurs when certain neural connections in the brain are strengthened—it is clear that both nurture and nature involve biological processes.

Scientists have made tremendous strides in treating depression. With the advent of such antidepressants as Prozac (which acts on the serotonergic system), more than 80 percent of depressed patients now respond to medication or psychotherapy, or a combination of the two. But much more work remains to be done. Because depression is so common, its cost to society is high. The National Institute of Mental Health estimates that depression claims $30.4 billion in treatment and in lost productivity from the U.S. economy every year.

And these costs are on the rise: depression is becoming more common in successive generations (the so-called cohort effect). No one knows what is causing the cohort effect—but it is moving much too quickly to have a genetic basis. Theories about what is causing the cohort effect range from increased drug abuse and familial disarray to the suggestion that perhaps older people are simply more likely to forget past depressive episodes when asked. The cohort effect and depression in general remain very much a mystery. And for the men and women who suffer from it, it is a mystery that cannot be solved soon enough. ▪

ELLEN LEIBENLUFT is chief of the Unit on Rapid Cycling Bipolar Disorder within the Clinical Psychobiology Branch at the National Institute of Mental Health.

Treating PMS with Antidepressants

From time to time, almost all women experience what is known as premenstrual syndrome (PMS): mild cramping, bloating, irritability and fatigue. For some, the symptoms preceding menstrual periods are debilitating. An estimated 3 to 5 percent of all women suffer from marked distress, anger, tension and mood swings every month. For these women a range of remedies—including progesterone, estrogen, diuretics, vitamins, herbs and mineral preparations—have proved useless.

The bad news is that no one has figured out exactly what causes the condition—which psychiatrists now call premenstrual dysmorphic disorder (PDD). But scientists have found that a class of antidepressants, called selective serotonin reuptake inhibitors (SSRIs), can alleviate PDD in some patients. These medications represent a big improvement over the only previous solution—surgically removing the ovaries. And the fact that these drugs help also underscores the point that PDD has a biochemical basis. It is not—as many women have been told by their physicians—something they imagine.

Most evidence suggests that women with PDD have deficiencies in the neurotransmitter serotonin. SSRIs, such as Prozac, Zoloft and Paxil, act in the brain to raise serotonin levels. Studies show that tryptophan, an amino acid the body uses to make serotonin, can relieve symptoms of PDD, and laboratory tests reveal that women with PDD have abnormal blood levels of serotonin. In addition, the disorder often causes women to crave carbohydrates, a symptom that is also associated with a dearth of serotonin.

Since SSRIs were introduced in the late 1980s, roughly a dozen studies have demonstrated their efficacy in treating PDD; last year a

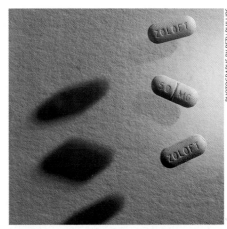

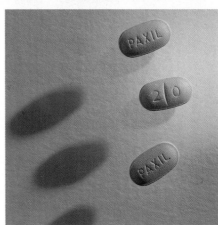

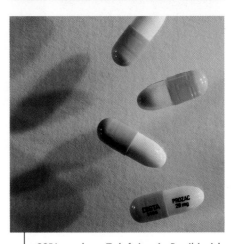

SSRIs such as Zoloft (top), Paxil (middle) and Prozac (bottom) help some women with severe PMS.

PHOTOGRAPHS BY BETH PHILLIPS

large investigation—involving more than 200 women and 12 medical centers—corroborated the finding. Kimberly Yonkers of the University of Texas Southwestern Medical Center at Dallas and her colleagues published in the *Journal of the American Medical Association* that 62 percent of women treated with the SSRI sertraline (Zoloft) improved, compared with only 34 percent of women who received a placebo. It is unclear whether SSRIs can alleviate less severe forms of PMS, but further research should lead to answers. —*Kristin Leutwyler, staff writer*

Manic-Depressive Illness and Creativity

Does some fine madness plague great artists?
Several studies now show that creativity
and mood disorders are linked

by Kay Redfield Jamison

Sylvia Plath

Paul Gauguin

Walt Whitman

Vincent van Gogh

Virginia Woolf

Gustav Mahler

Cole Porter

Anne Sexton

John Berryman

Edgar Allan Poe

"Men have called me mad," wrote Edgar Allan Poe, "but the question is not yet settled, whether madness is or is not the loftiest intelligence—whether much that is glorious—whether all that is profound—does not spring from disease of thought—from moods of mind exalted at the expense of the general intellect."

Many people have long shared Poe's suspicion that genius and insanity are entwined. Indeed, history holds countless examples of "that fine madness." Scores of influential 18th- and 19th-century poets, notably William Blake, Lord Byron and Alfred, Lord Tennyson, wrote about the extreme mood swings they endured. Modern American poets John Berryman, Randall Jarrell, Robert Lowell, Sylvia Plath, Theodore Roethke, Delmore Schwartz and Anne Sexton were all hospitalized for either mania or depression during their lives. And many painters and composers, among them Vincent van Gogh, Georgia O'Keeffe, Charles Mingus and Robert Schumann, have been similarly afflicted.

Judging by current diagnostic criteria, it seems that most of these artists—and many others besides—suffered from one of the major mood disorders, namely, manic-depressive illness or major depression. Both are fairly common, very treatable and yet frequently lethal diseases. Major depression induces intense melancholic spells, whereas manic-depression, a strongly genetic disease,

WRITERS, ARTISTS AND COMPOSERS shown in this montage all most likely suffered from manic-depressive illness or major depressive illness, according to their letters and journals, medical records and accounts by their families and friends. Recent studies indicate that the temperaments and cognitive styles associated with mood disorders can in fact enhance creativity in some individuals.

Hermann Hesse

Samuel Clemens (Mark Twain)

BETTMANN ARCHIVE

Tennessee Williams

GRANGER COLLECTION

BETTMANN ARCHIVE

Mark Rothko

MAN RAY *Granger Collection*

UPI/BETTMANN

Charles Mingus

AP/ WIDE WORLD PHOTOS

Ezra Pound

Ernest Hemingway

GRANGER COLLECTION

Georgia O'Keeffe

ROBERT CAPA *Magnum*

UPI/BETTMANN NEWSPHOTOS

HENRI CARTIER-BRESSON *Magnum*

The Tainted Blood of the Tennysons

Alfred, Lord Tennyson, who experienced recurrent, debilitating depressions and probable hypomanic spells, often expressed fear that he might inherit the madness, or "taint of blood," in his family. His father, grandfather, two of his great-grandfathers as well as five of his seven brothers suffered from insanity, melancholia, uncontrollable rage or what is today known as manic-depressive illness. His brother Edward was confined to an asylum for nearly 60 years before he died from manic exhaustion. Lionel Tennyson, one of Alfred's two sons, displayed a mercurial temperament, as did one of his three grandsons.

Modern medicine has confirmed that manic-depression and creativity tend to run in certain families. Studies of twins provide strong evidence for the heritability of manic-depressive illness. If an identical twin has manic-depressive illness, the other twin has a 70 to 100 percent chance of also having the disease; if the other twin is fraternal, the chances are considerably lower (approximately 20 percent). A review of identical twins reared apart from birth—in which at least one of the twins had been diagnosed as manic-depressive—found that two thirds or more of the sets were concordant for the illness.

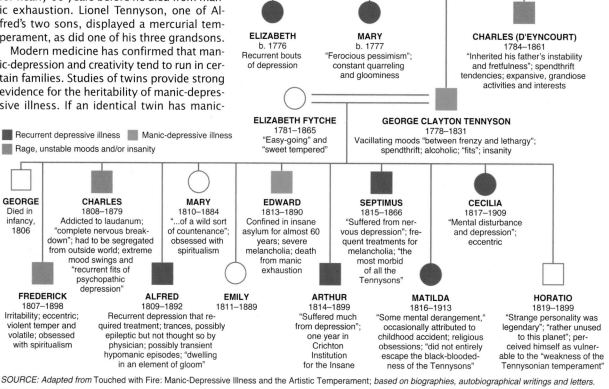

■ Recurrent depressive illness   ■ Manic-depressive illness
■ Rage, unstable moods and/or insanity

ELIZABETH
b. 1776
Recurrent bouts of depression

MARY
b. 1777
"Ferocious pessimism"; constant quarreling and gloominess

CHARLES (D'EYNCOURT)
1784–1861
"Inherited his father's instability and fretfulness"; spendthrift tendencies; expansive, grandiose activities and interests

ELIZABETH FYTCHE
1781–1865
"Easy-going" and "sweet tempered"

GEORGE CLAYTON TENNYSON
1778–1831
Vacillating moods "between frenzy and lethargy"; spendthrift; alcoholic; "fits"; insanity

GEORGE
Died in infancy, 1806

CHARLES
1808–1879
Addicted to laudanum; "complete nervous breakdown"; had to be segregated from outside world; extreme mood swings and "recurrent fits of psychopathic depression"

MARY
1810–1884
"...of a wild sort of countenance"; obsessed with spiritualism

EDWARD
1813–1890
Confined in insane asylum for almost 60 years; severe melancholia; death from manic exhaustion

SEPTIMUS
1815–1866
"Suffered from nervous depression"; frequent treatments for melancholia; "the most morbid of all the Tennysons"

CECILIA
1817–1909
"Mental disturbance and depression"; eccentric

FREDERICK
1807–1898
Irritability; eccentric; violent temper and volatile; obsessed with spiritualism

ALFRED
1809–1892
Recurrent depression that required treatment; trances, possibly epileptic but not thought so by physician; possibly transient hypomanic episodes; "dwelling in an element of gloom"

EMILY
1811–1889

ARTHUR
1814–1899
"Suffered much from depression"; one year in Crichton Institution for the Insane

MATILDA
1816–1913
"Some mental derangement," occasionally attributed to childhood accident; religious obsessions; "did not entirely escape the black-bloodedness of the Tennysons"

HORATIO
1819–1899
"Strange personality was legendary"; "rather unused to this planet"; perceived himself as vulnerable to the "weakness of the Tennysonian temperament"

SOURCE: Adapted from Touched with Fire: Manic-Depressive Illness and the Artistic Temperament; based on biographies, autobiographical writings and letters.

LISA BURNETT

---

pitches patients repeatedly from depressed to hyperactive and euphoric, or intensely irritable, states. In its milder form, termed cyclothymia, manic-depression causes pronounced but not totally debilitating changes in mood, behavior, sleep, thought patterns and energy levels. Advanced cases are marked by dramatic, cyclic shifts.

Could such disruptive diseases convey certain creative advantages? Many people find that proposition counterintuitive. Most manic-depressives do not possess extraordinary imagination, and most accomplished artists do not suffer from recurring mood swings. To assume, then, that such diseases usually promote artistic talent wrongly reinforces simplistic notions of the "mad genius." Worse yet, such a generalization trivializes a very serious medical condition and, to some degree, discredits individuality in the arts as well. It would be wrong to label anyone who is unusually accomplished, energetic, intense, moody or eccentric as manic-depressive.

All the same, recent studies indicate that a high number of established artists—far more than could be expected by chance—meet the diagnostic criteria for manic-depression or major depression given in the fourth edition of the *Diagnostic and Statistical Manual of Mental Disorders* (*DSM-IV*). In fact, it seems that these diseases can sometimes enhance or otherwise contribute to creativity in some people.

Diagnosing Mood Disorders

By virtue of their prevalence alone, it is clear that mood disorders do not necessarily breed genius. Indeed, 1 percent of the general population suffer from manic-depression, also called bipolar disorder, and 5 percent from a major depression, or unipolar disorder, during their lifetime. Depression affects twice as many women as men and most often, but not always, strikes later in life. Bipolar disorder afflicts equal numbers of women and men, and more than a third of all cases surface before age 20. Some 60 to 80 percent of all adolescents and adults who commit suicide have a history of bipolar or unipolar illness. Before the late 1970s, when the drug lithium first became widely available, one person in five with manic-depression committed suicide.

Major depression in both unipolar and bipolar disorders manifests itself through apathy, lethargy, hopelessness, sleep disturbances, slowed physical movements and thinking, impaired memory and concentration, and a loss of pleasure in typically enjoyable events. The diagnostic criteria also include suicidal thinking, self-blame and inappropriate guilt. To distinguish clinical depression from normal periods of unhappiness, the common guidelines further require that these symptoms persist for a minimum of two to four weeks and also that they significantly interfere with a person's everyday functioning.

During episodes of mania or hypomania (mild mania), bipolar patients experience symptoms that are in many ways the opposite of those associated with depression. Their mood and self-esteem are elevated. They sleep less and have abundant energy; their productivity increases. Manics frequently become paranoid and irritable. Moreover, their speech is often rapid, excitable and intrusive, and their thoughts move quickly and fluidly from one topic to another. They usually hold tremendous conviction about the correctness and importance of their own ideas as well. This grandiosity can contribute to poor judgment and impulsive behavior.

Hypomanics and manics generally have chaotic personal and professional relationships. They may spend large sums of money, drive recklessly or pursue questionable business ventures or sexual liaisons. In some cases, manics suffer from violent agitation and delusional thoughts as well as visual and auditory hallucinations.

Rates of Mood Disorders

For years, scientists have documented some kind of connection between mania, depression and creative output. In the late 19th and early 20th centuries, researchers turned to accounts of mood disorders written by prominent artists, their physicians and friends. Although largely anecdotal, this work strongly suggested that renowned writers, artists and composers—and their first-degree relatives—were far more likely to experience mood disorders and

KAY REDFIELD JAMISON is professor of psychiatry at the Johns Hopkins University School of Medicine. She wrote *Touched with Fire: Manic-Depressive Illness and the Artistic Temperament* and co-authored the medical text *Manic-Depressive Illness*. Jamison is a member of the National Advisory Council for Human Genome Research and clinical director of the Dana Consortium on the Genetic Basis of Manic-Depressive Illness. She has also written and produced a series of public television specials about manic-depressive illness and the arts.

to commit suicide than was the general population. During the past 20 years, more systematic studies of artistic populations have confirmed these findings [*see illustration below*]. Diagnostic and psychological analyses of living writers and artists can give quite meaningful estimates of the rates and types of psychopathology they experience.

In the 1970s Nancy C. Andreasen of the University of Iowa completed the first of these rigorous studies, which made use of structured interviews, matched control groups and strict diagnostic criteria. She examined 30 creative writers and found an extraordinarily high occurrence of mood disorders and alcoholism among them. Eighty percent had experienced at least one episode of major depression, hypomania or mania; 43 percent reported a history of hypomania or mania. Also, the relatives of these writers, compared with the relatives of the control subjects, generally performed more creative work and more often had a mood disorder.

A few years later, while on sabbatical in England from the University of California at Los Angeles, I began a study of 47 distinguished British writers and visual artists. To select the group as best I could for creativity, I purposefully

chose painters and sculptors who were Royal Academicians or Associates of the Royal Academy. All the playwrights had won the New York Drama Critics Award or the Evening Standard Drama (London Critics) Award, or both. Half of the poets were already represented in the *Oxford Book of Twentieth Century English Verse*. I found that 38 percent of these artists and writers had in fact been previously treated for a mood disorder; three fourths of those treated had required medication or hospitalization, or both. And half of the poets—the largest fraction from any one group—had needed such extensive care.

Hagop S. Akiskal of the University of California at San Diego, also affiliated with the University of Tennessee at Memphis, and his wife, Kareen Akiskal, subsequently interviewed 20 award-winning European writers, poets, painters and sculptors. Some two thirds of their subjects exhibited recurrent cyclothymic or hypomanic tendencies, and half had at one time suffered from a major depression. In collaboration with David H. Evans of the University of Memphis, the Akiskals noted the same trends among living blues musicians. More recently Stuart A. Montgomery and his wife, Deirdre B. Montgomery, of St.

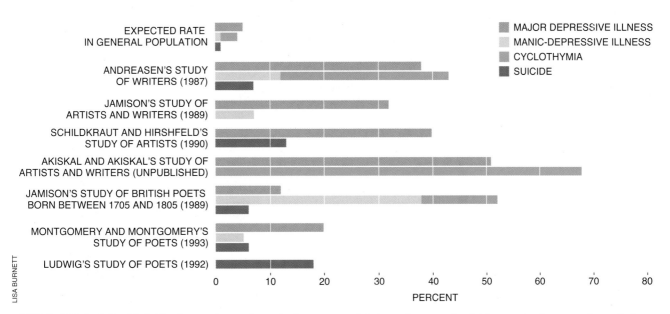

INCREASED RATES of suicide, depression and manic-depression among artists have been established by many separate studies. These investigations show that artists experience up to 18 times the rate of suicide seen in the general population, eight to 10 times the rate of depression and 10 to 20 times the rate of manic-depression and cyclothymia.

Mary's Hospital in London examined 50 modern British poets. One fourth met current diagnostic criteria for depression or manic-depression; suicide was six times more frequent in this community than in the general population.

Ruth L. Richards and her colleagues at Harvard University set up a system for assessing the degree of original thinking required to perform certain creative tasks. Then, rather than screening for mood disorders among those already deemed highly inventive, they attempted to rate creativity in a sample of manic-depressive patients. Based on their scale, they found that compared with individuals having no personal or family history of psychiatric disorders, manic-depressive and cyclothymic patients (as well as their unaffected relatives) showed greater creativity.

Biographical studies of earlier generations of artists and writers also show consistently high rates of suicide, depression and manic-depression—up to 18 times the rate of suicide seen in the general population, eight to 10 times that of depression and 10 to 20 times that of manic-depressive illness and its milder variants. Joseph J. Schildkraut and his co-workers at Harvard concluded that approximately half of the 15 20th-century abstract-expressionist artists they studied suffered from depressive or manic-depressive illness; the suicide rate in this group was at least 13 times the current U.S. national rate.

In 1992 Arnold M. Ludwig of the University of Kentucky published an extensive biographical survey of 1,005 famous 20th-century artists, writers and other professionals, some of whom had been in treatment for a mood disorder. He discovered that the artists and writers experienced two to three times the rate of psychosis, suicide attempts, mood disorders and substance abuse than did comparably successful people in business, science and public life. The poets in this sample had most often been manic or psychotic and hospitalized; they also proved to be some 18 times more likely to commit suicide than is the general public. In a comprehensive biographical study of 36 major British poets born between 1705 and 1805, I found similarly elevated rates of psychosis and severe psychopathology. These poets were 30 times more likely to have had manic-depressive illness than were their contemporaries, at least 20 times more likely to have been committed to an asylum and some five times more likely to have taken their own life.

Cycles of Creative Accomplishment

These corroborative studies have confirmed that highly creative individuals experience major mood disorders more often than do other groups in the general population. But what does this mean for their work? How does a psychiatric illness actually contribute to creative achievement? First, the common features of hypomania seem highly conducive to original thinking; the diagnostic criteria for this phase of the disorder include "sharpened and unusually creative thinking and increased productivity." And accumulating evidence suggests that the cognitive styles associated with hypomania (namely, expansive thought and grandiose moods) can lead to increased fluency and frequency of thoughts.

Studying the speech of hypomanic patients has revealed that they tend to rhyme and use other sound associations, such as alliteration, far more often than do unaffected individuals. They also use idiosyncratic words nearly three times as often as do control subjects. Moreover, in specific drills, they can list synonyms or form other word associations much more rapidly than is considered normal. It seems, then, that both the quantity and quality of thoughts build during hypomania. This speed increase may range from a very mild quickening to complete psychotic incoherence. It is not yet clear what causes this qualitative change in mental processing. Nevertheless, this altered cognitive state may well facilitate the formation of unique ideas and associations.

Manic-depressive illness and creative accomplishment share certain noncognitive features: the ability to function well on a few hours of sleep, the focus needed to work intensively, bold and restless attitudes, and an ability to experience a profound depth and variety of emotions. The less dramatic daily aspects of manic-depression might also provide creative advantage to some individuals. The manic-depressive temperament is, in a biological sense, an alert, sensitive system that reacts strongly and swiftly. It responds to the world

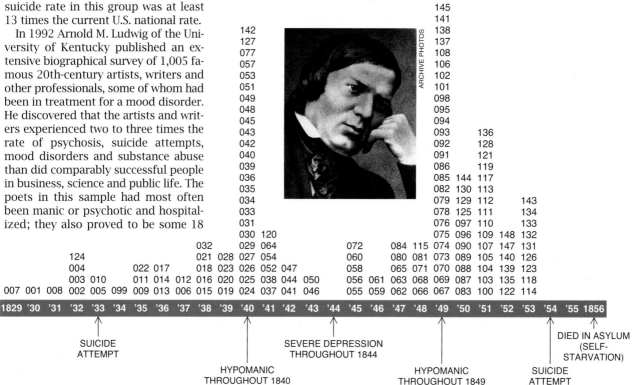

ROBERT SCHUMANN'S MUSICAL WORKS, charted by year and opus number (*above*), show a striking relation between his mood states and his productivity. He composed the most when hypomanic and the least when depressed. Both of Schumann's parents were clinically depressed, and two other first-degree relatives committed suicide. Schumann himself attempted suicide twice and died in an insane asylum. One of his sons spent more than 30 years in a mental institution.

The Case of Vincent van Gogh

Many clinicians have reviewed the medical and psychiatric problems of the painter Vincent van Gogh posthumously, diagnosing him with a range of disorders, including epilepsy, schizophrenia, digitalis and absinthe poisoning, manic-depressive psychosis, acute intermittent porphyria and Ménière's disease. Richard Jed Wyatt of the National Institute of Mental Health and the author have argued in detail that van Gogh's symptoms, the natural course of his illness and his family psychiatric history strongly indicate manic-depressive illness. The extent of the artist's purported absinthe use and convulsive behavior remains unclear; in any event, his psychiatric symptoms long predate any possible history of seizures. It is possible that he suffered from both epilepsy and manic-depressive illness.

Irises, 1889

with a wide range of emotional, perceptual, intellectual, behavioral and energy changes. In a sense, depression is a view of the world through a dark glass, and mania is that seen through a kaleidoscope—often brilliant but fractured.

Where depression questions, ruminates and hesitates, mania answers with vigor and certainty. The constant transitions in and out of constricted and then expansive thoughts, subdued and then violent responses, grim and then ebullient moods, withdrawn and then outgoing stances, cold and then fiery states—and the rapidity and fluidity of moves through such contrasting experiences—can be painful and confusing. Ideally, though, such chaos in those able to transcend it or shape it to their will can provide a familiarity with transitions that is probably useful in artistic endeavors. This vantage readily accepts ambiguities and the counteracting forces in nature.

Extreme changes in mood exaggerate the normal tendency to have conflicting selves; the undulating, rhythmic and transitional moods and cognitive changes so characteristic of manic-depressive illness can blend or harness seemingly contradictory moods, observations and perceptions. Ultimately, these fluxes and yokings may reflect truth in humanity and nature more accurately than could a more fixed viewpoint. The "consistent attitude toward life," may not, as Byron scholar Jerome J. McGann of the University of Virginia points out, be as insightful as an ability to live with, and portray, constant change.

The ethical and societal implications of the association between mood disorders and creativity are important but poorly understood. Some treatment strategies pay insufficient heed to the benefits manic-depressive illness can bestow on some individuals. Certainly most manic-depressives seek relief from the disease, and lithium and anticonvulsant drugs are very effective therapies for manias and depressions. Nevertheless, these drugs can dampen a person's general intellect and limit his or her emotional and perceptual range. For this reason, many manic-depressive patients stop taking these medications.

Left untreated, however, manic-depressive illness often worsens over time—and no one is creative when severely depressed, psychotic or dead. The attacks of both mania and depression tend to grow more frequent and more severe. Without regular treatment the disease eventually becomes less responsive to medication. In addition, bipolar and unipolar patients frequently abuse mood-altering substances, such as alcohol and illicit drugs, both of which can cause secondary medical and emotional burdens for manic-depressive and depressed patients.

The Goal of Treatment

The real task of imaginative, compassionate and effective treatment, therefore, is to give patients more meaningful choices than they are now afforded. Useful intervention must control the extremes of depression and psychosis without sacrificing crucial human emotions and experiences. Given time and increasingly sophisticated research, psychiatrists will likely gain a better understanding of the complex biological basis for mood disorders. Eventually, the development of new drugs should make it possible to treat manic-depressive individuals so that those aspects of temperament and cognition that are essential to the creative process remain intact.

The development of more specific and less problematic therapies should be swift once scientists find the gene, or genes, responsible for the disease. Prenatal tests and other diagnostic measures may then become available; these possibilities raise a host of complicated ethical issues. It would be irresponsible to romanticize such a painful, destructive and all too often deadly disease. Hence, 3 to 5 percent of the Human Genome Project's total budget (which is conservatively estimated at $3 billion) has been set aside for studies of the social, ethical and legal implications of genetic research. It is hoped that these investigations will examine the troubling issues surrounding manic-depression and major depression at length. To help those who have manic-depressive illness, or who are at risk for it, must be a major public health priority.

FURTHER READING

TENNYSON: THE UNQUIET HEART. R. B. Martin. Oxford University Press, 1980.

CREATIVITY AND MENTAL ILLNESS: PREVALENCE RATES IN WRITERS AND THEIR FIRST-DEGREE RELATIVES. Nancy C. Andreasen in *American Journal of Psychiatry,* Vol. 144, No. 10, pages 1288-1292; October 1987.

MANIC DEPRESSIVE ILLNESS. Frederick K. Goodwin and Kay R. Jamison. Oxford University Press, 1990.

CREATIVE ACHIEVEMENT AND PSYCHOPATHOLOGY: COMPARISON AMONG PROFESSIONS. Arnold M. Ludwig in *American Journal of Psychotherapy,* Vol. 46, No. 3, pages 330–356; July 1992.

TOUCHED WITH FIRE: MANIC-DEPRESSIVE ILLNESS AND THE ARTISTIC TEMPERAMENT. Kay R. Jamison. Free Press/Macmillan, 1993.

The Puzzle of Hypertension in African-Americans

by Richard S. Cooper, Charles N. Rotimi and Ryk Ward

Nearly all Americans undergo a steady rise in blood pressure with age. Almost 25 percent cross the line into hypertension, the technical term for chronically high blood pressure. This condition, in turn, can silently contribute to heart disease, stroke and kidney failure and thus plays a part in some 500,000 deaths every year. For black Americans, the situation is even more dire: 35 percent suffer from hypertension. Worse, the ailment is particularly deadly in this population,

DANIELS & DANIELS

YORAM LEHMANN *Peter Arnold, Inc.*

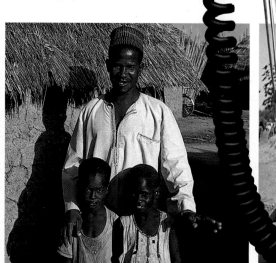

YORAM LEHMANN *Peter Arnold, Inc.*

TOMPIX *Peter Arnold, Inc.*

Genes are often invoked to account for why high blood pressure is so common among African-Americans. Yet the rates are low in Africans. This discrepancy demonstrates how genes and the environment interact

accounting for 20 percent of deaths among blacks in the U.S.—twice the figure for whites.

One popular explanation of this disparity between blacks and whites holds that people of African descent are "intrinsically susceptible" to high blood pressure because of some vaguely defined aspect of their genetic makeup. This conclusion is not satisfying. Indeed, the answer troubles us, for as we will show, it does not reflect the available evidence accurately. Instead such reasoning appears to follow from the racialized character of much public health research, which at times defaults to reductionist interpretations that emphasize the importance of racial or genetic characteristics. Race be-

comes the underlying cause for the presence of a disease, rather than being recognized as a proxy for many other variables (along the lines of, say, socioeconomic status) that influence the course of a disorder.

We suggest that a more fruitful approach to understanding the high levels of hypertension among African-Americans would begin by abandoning conventional hypotheses about

INCIDENCE OF HYPERTENSION, or chronic high blood pressure, was assessed by the authors in Africans as well as in people of African descent in the U.S. and the Caribbean. The rate dropped dramatically from the U.S. across the Atlantic to Africa (*graph*), and the difference was most pronounced between urban African-Americans (*below, right*) and rural Nigerians (*below, left*). The findings suggest that hypertension may largely be a disease of modern life and that genes alone do not account for the high rates of hypertension in African-Americans.

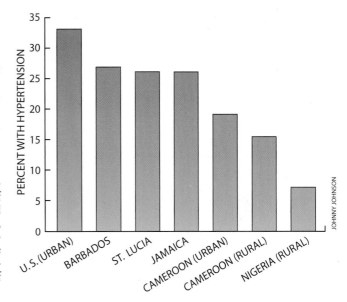

JOHNNY JOHNSON

JIM SUGAR PHOTOGRAPHY *Corbis*

DONNA BINDER *Impact Visuals*

CHRISTOPHER SMITH *Impact Visuals*

The Puzzle of Hypertension in African-Americans

What Pressure Readings Mean

Blood pressure is measured with a sphygmomanometer, which gives a reading of two numbers: systolic and diastolic pressure. The systolic reading indicates the maximum pressure exerted by the blood on the arterial walls; this high point occurs when the left ventricle of the heart contracts, forcing blood through the arteries. Diastolic pressure is a measure of the lowest pressure on the blood vessel walls and happens when the left ventricle relaxes and refills with blood. Healthy blood pressure is considered to be around 120 millimeters of mercury systolic, 80 millimeters of mercury diastolic (usually presented as 120/80).

Many people can experience temporary increases in blood pressure, particularly under stressful conditions. When blood pressure is consistently above 140/90, however, physicians diagnose hypertension. The disorder can generally be managed with the help of special diets, exercise regimens and medication. —*The Editors*

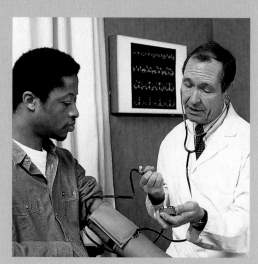

race. It would acknowledge that hypertension arises through many different pathways, involving complex interactions among external factors (such as stress or diet), internal physiology (the biological systems that regulate blood pressure) and the genes involved in controlling blood pressure. Only by teasing out the connections among all three tiers of this model will scientists truly comprehend how high blood pressure develops. This knowledge will then enable researchers to return successfully to the questions of why the disorder is so prevalent among African-Americans and how best to intervene for all patients.

One strategy for clarifying the relative significance of different environmental factors would be to hold constant the genetic background of people in distinct environments and focus on the variations in their living conditions or behavior. This kind of experiment is impossible to do perfectly, particularly when vast numbers of Americans have at least one, and frequently several, of the known behavioral risk factors for developing high blood pressure: being overweight, eating a high-salt diet, suffering long-term psychological stress,

being physically inactive and drinking alcohol to excess. In a way, the situation is analogous to trying to identify the causes of lung cancer in a society where everyone smokes; without having nonsmokers for a comparison group, researchers would never know that smoking contributes so profoundly to lung cancer.

Lessons from the Past

Our solution to this dilemma was to turn to Africa. In 1991 we initiated a research project concentrated on the African diaspora, the forced migration of West Africans between the 16th and 19th centuries. In this shameful chapter of world history, European slave traders on the west coast of Africa purchased or captured an estimated 10 million people and transported them to the Caribbean and the Americas, where they gradually mixed with Europeans and Native Americans. Today their descendants live throughout the Western Hemisphere.

Scientists have known for some time that the rate of hypertension in rural West Africa is lower than in any other place in the world, except for some

parts of the Amazon basin and the South Pacific. People of African descent in the U.S. and the U.K., on the other hand, have among the highest rates of hypertension in the world. This shift suggests that something about the surroundings or way of life of European and American blacks—rather than a genetic factor—was the fundamental cause of their altered susceptibility to high blood pressure.

To elucidate what was triggering hypertension among these people, we established research facilities in communities in Nigeria, Cameroon, Zimbabwe, St. Lucia, Barbados, Jamaica and the U.S. As the project progressed, we focused our attention on Nigeria, Jamaica and the U.S. as the three countries that allow us, in a sense, to capture the medical effects of the westward movement of Africans from their native lands. We conducted testing of randomly sampled people at each location to determine the general prevalence of both hypertension and its common risk factors, such as eating a high-salt diet or being obese or physically inactive.

As might be expected, the differences between the three societies are vast. The Nigerian community we surveyed, with the help of colleagues at the University of Ibadan Medical School, is a rural one in the district of Igbo-Ora. Polygamy is a common practice there, so families tend to be complex and large; on average, women raise five children. The residents of Igbo-Ora are typically lean, engage in physically demanding subsistence farming and eat the traditional Nigerian diet of rice, tubers and fruit.

Nations in sub-Saharan Africa do not keep formal records on mortality and life expectancy, but based on local studies, we assume that infection, especially malaria, is the major killer. Our research revealed that adults in Igbo-Ora have an annual mortality risk of between 1 and 2 percent—high by any Western standard. Those who do survive to older ages tend to be quite healthy. In particular, blood pressure does not rise with age, and even though hypertension does occur, it is rare. (We were pleased that we could coordinate with the established medical personnel in the region to treat those patients who did suffer from hypertension.)

Jamaica, in contrast, is an emerging industrial economy in which the risk of infectious disease is very low but the levels of chronic disease are higher than

The Puzzle of Hypertension in African-Americans

in Nigeria. The base of operations for our team was Spanish Town, the original colonial capital of Jamaica. A bustling city of 90,000 people, Spanish Town features a cross section of Jamaican society. Investigators at the Tropical Metabolism Research Unit of the University of the West Indies, Mona Campus, led the project.

The family structure in Jamaica has evolved away from the patriarchy of Africa. Women head a significant number of households, which are generally small and often fragmented. Chronic unemployment has tended to marginalize men and lower their social position. Farming and other physically demanding occupations are common; residents' diets include a blend of local foodstuffs and modern commercial products. Despite widespread poverty, life expectancy in Jamaica is six years longer than it is for blacks in the U.S. because of lower rates of cardiovascular disease and cancer.

In the metropolitan Chicago area, we worked in the primarily African-American city of Maywood. Many of the older adults in this community were born in the southern U.S., primarily in Mississippi, Alabama or Arkansas. Interestingly, the northern migration seems to have greatly improved both the health and the economic standing of these people. Unionized jobs in heavy industry provide the best opportunities for men, whereas women have been integrated into the workforce across a range of job categories. The prevailing diet is typical American fare: high in fat and salt. The generation now reaching late adulthood has enjoyed substantial increases in life expectancy, although progress has been uneven in the past decade.

Similarities and Differences

Even as we sought out these examples of contrasting cultures, we were careful to make sure the people we studied had similar genetic backgrounds. We found that the American and Jamaican blacks who participated shared, on average, 75 percent of their genetic heritage with the Nigerians. Against this common genetic background, a number of important differences stood out.

First, the rates of hypertension: just 7 percent of the group in rural Nigeria had high blood pressure, with increased rates noted in urban areas. Around 26 percent of the black Jamaicans and 33

percent of the black Americans surveyed were either suffering from hypertension or already taking medication to lower their blood pressure. In addition, certain risk factors for high blood pressure became more common as we moved across the Atlantic. Body mass index, a measure of weight relative to height, went up steadily from Africa to Jamaica to the U.S., as did average salt intake. Our analysis of these data suggests that being overweight, and the associated lack of exercise and poor diet, explains between 40 and 50 percent of the increased risk for hypertension that African-Americans face compared with Nigerians. Variations in dietary salt intake are likely to contribute to the excess risk as well.

The African diaspora has turned out to be a powerful tool for evaluating the effects of a changing society and environment on a relatively stable gene pool. Our study also raises the question of whether rising blood pressure is a nearly unavoidable hazard of modern

life for people of all skin colors. The human cardiovascular system evolved in the geographic setting of rural Africa in which obesity was uncommon, salt intake was moderate, the diet was low in fat, and high levels of physical activity were required. The life of subsistence farmers in Africa today has not, at least in these respects, changed all that much. We see that for people living this

> *The African diaspora has turned out to be a powerful tool for evaluating the effects of a changing society and environment.*

way, blood pressure hardly rises with age and atherosclerosis is virtually unknown. As a result, the African farmers provide epidemiologists with a revealing control group that can be compared with populations living in more modernized societies.

It is disquieting to recognize that a modest shift from these baseline conditions leads to sizable changes in the risk for hypertension. For instance, blood pressures are substantially higher in the

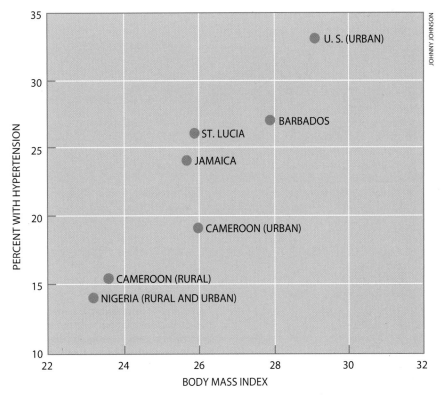

BODY MASS INDEX, or BMI, measures a person's weight-to-height ratio; a BMI over 25 is generally considered a sign of being overweight. In the authors' study of people of African descent, a low average BMI in a population corresponded to a low rate of hypertension in that community. As average BMI increased, so did the prevalence of hypertension. The findings support the view that obesity contributes to high blood pressure.

city of Ibadan, Nigeria, than in nearby rural areas, despite small differences in the groups' overall levels of obesity and sodium intake. Other variables, such as psychological stress and lack of physical activity, may help account for this increase.

Psychological and social stresses are extremely difficult to measure, especially across cultures. Yet there is little dispute that blacks in North America and Europe face a unique kind of stress—racial discrimination. The long-term effects of racism on blood pressure remain unknown; however, it is worth noting that blacks in certain parts of the Caribbean, including Trinidad, Cuba and rural Puerto Rico, have average blood pressures that are nearly the same as those of other racial groups. Although this is no more than conjec-

ture, perhaps the relationships among races in those societies impose fewer insults on the cardiovascular system than those in the continental U.S. do.

Environment at Work

As epidemiologists, we want to move beyond these descriptive findings of what might increase people's risk for hypertension and examine more closely how environmental and biological risk factors interact to produce the disease. Physiologists have not yet uncovered every detail of how the body regulates blood pressure. Nevertheless, they know that the kidneys play a key role, by controlling the concentration in the bloodstream of sodium ions (derived from table salt—sodium chloride—in the diet), which in turn influ-

ences blood volume and blood pressure.

Having evolved when the human diet was habitually low in sodium, the kidneys developed an enormous capacity to retain this vital ion. As these organs filter waste from the blood, they routinely hold on to as much as 98 percent of the sodium that passes through, then eventually return the ion to the bloodstream. When doused with sodium, however, the kidneys will excrete excessive amounts into the blood, thereby elevating blood pressure. Too much salt in the kidneys can also harm their internal filtering mechanism, leading to a sustained rise in pressure.

As a gauge of how well the organs were modulating the body's sodium balance in our patients, we decided to measure the activity of an important biochemical pathway that helps to reg-

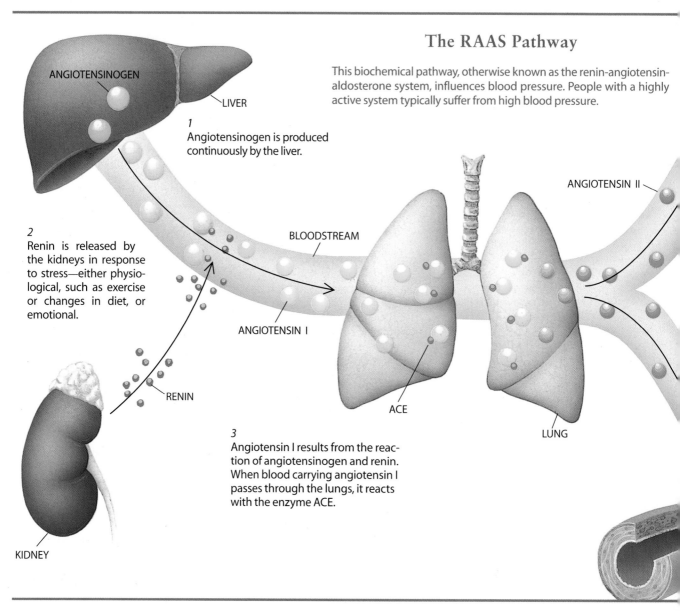

The RAAS Pathway

This biochemical pathway, otherwise known as the renin-angiotensin-aldosterone system, influences blood pressure. People with a highly active system typically suffer from high blood pressure.

ANGIOTENSINOGEN

LIVER

1
Angiotensinogen is produced continuously by the liver.

2
Renin is released by the kidneys in response to stress—either physiological, such as exercise or changes in diet, or emotional.

RENIN

KIDNEY

BLOODSTREAM

ANGIOTENSIN I

ACE

ANGIOTENSIN II

LUNG

3
Angiotensin I results from the reaction of angiotensinogen and renin. When blood carrying angiotensin I passes through the lungs, it reacts with the enzyme ACE.

TOMO NARASHIMA

ulate blood pressure. Known as the renin-angiotensin-aldosterone system, or RAAS, this intricate series of chemical reactions (named for three of the compounds involved) has the net effect of controlling the amount of the protein angiotensin II present in the bloodstream. Angiotensin II performs a range of functions, such as prompting the constriction of blood vessels, which causes a rise in blood pressure, and triggering the release of another crucial chemical, aldosterone, which induces an increase in the reuptake of sodium by the kidneys. In short, a highly active RAAS pathway should correlate with elevated blood pressure.

As a convenient method for tracing the activity of RAAS in our patients, we measured the amount of the compound angiotensinogen—one of the chemicals involved in the first step of RAAS [see *illustration below*]—present in blood samples. One advantage to measuring angiotensinogen is that unlike other, short-lived compounds in the pathway, it circulates at a relatively constant level in the bloodstream.

As expected, we found that in general the higher angiotensinogen levels are, the higher blood pressure is likely to be, although this association is not as strong for women (variations in estrogen also appear to affect a woman's blood pressure). Further, the average level of angiotensinogen for each group we studied increased substantially as we moved from Nigeria to Jamaica to the U.S., just as the rate of hypertension did; that pattern was found in both men and women.

Our results suggest that some of the risk factors for hypertension might promote the disorder by elevating levels of angiotensinogen in the blood. Obesity, in particular, may contribute to chronic high blood pressure in this way. Excessive body fat, for instance, has been shown to correspond to an elevation in an individual's circulating level of angiotensinogen. And the incidence of obesity rose more or less in parallel with levels of hypertension and angiotensinogen in our study groups. Correlations do not necessarily prove causality, of course, but the collected findings do hint that obesity promotes hypertension at least in part by leading to enhanced angiotensinogen production.

Clues in the Genes

Genetic findings seem to lend some support to a role for excess angiotensinogen in the development of hypertension. Scientists have found that some people carry certain variations of the gene for producing angiotensinogen (these variations in genes are known as alleles) that give rise to elevated levels of the protein. Intriguingly, people with these alleles tend to have a higher risk of developing high blood pressure.

Several years ago researchers at the University of Utah and the Collège de France in Paris reported that two alleles of the angiotensinogen gene, known as 235T and 174M, correlated with high levels of circulating angiotensinogen—as well as with hypertension—among people of European descent. The scientists do not know, however, whether these alleles themselves play a part in controlling angiotensinogen levels or are merely markers inherited along with other alleles that have more of an effect.

We must emphasize that identification of a gene associated with greater susceptibility to hypertension is not equivalent to finding the cause of the condition. Nor is it equivalent to saying that

The destructive effects of racism complicate any study of how a disease such as hypertension affects minority groups.

certain groups with the gene are fated to become hypertensive. Investigators have determined that genetic factors account for 25 to 40 percent of the variability in blood pressure between people and that many genes—perhaps as many as 10 or 15—can play a part in this variation. Those numbers indicate, then, that an isolated gene contributes only about 2 to 4 percent of the differences in blood pressure among people. And whether genes promote the development of hypertension depends considerably on whether the environmental influences needed to "express" those hypertension-causing traits are present.

Our own genetic findings seem to illustrate this point. In a quite perplexing discovery, we found that the 235T allele is twice as common among African-Americans as it is among European-Americans but that blacks with this form of the gene do not seem to be at an increased risk for hypertension compared with other blacks who do not carry the gene. Among the Nigerians in our study, we did see a modest elevation in levels of angiotensinogen in those with the 235T gene variant; again, however, this factor did not translate into a higher risk for hypertension. Furthermore, 90 percent of the Africans we tested carried the 235T allele, yet the rate of hypertension in this community is, as noted earlier, extremely low. (The frequency of the 174M allele was equivalent in all groups.)

It may well be that high angiotensinogen levels are not sufficient to trigger hypertension in people of African descent; rather other factors—genetic, physiological or environmental—may also be needed to induce the disorder. Alterna-

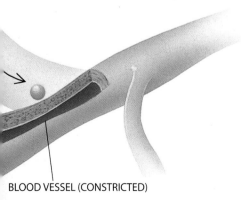

ADRENAL GLANDS

ALDOSTERONE

5
Aldosterone tells the kidney to take up salt and water from the bloodstream, thereby raising blood pressure.

4
Angiotensin II results from the reaction of angiotensin I and ACE. Angiotensin II has two primary effects. It prompts the adrenal glands to release aldosterone, and it causes smooth muscle in blood vessels to contract, which raises blood pressure.

BLOOD VESSEL (CONSTRICTED)

tively, this particular allele may not be equally important in the development of hypertension for all ethnic groups.

Pieces of the Puzzle

Although our results reveal at least one aspect of how nurture may interact with nature to alter a person's physiology and thereby produce hypertension, the findings also highlight the pitfalls of making sweeping generalizations. Clearly, no single allele and no single environmental factor can explain why hypertension occurs and why it is so common in African-Americans. An individual with a given mix of alleles may be susceptible to high blood pressure, but as our research on the African diaspora emphasizes, that person will develop hypertension only in a certain setting. The continuing challenge for researchers is to isolate specific genetic and environmental effects on hypertension and then put the pieces back together to determine the myriad ways these factors can conspire to cause chronic elevations of blood pressure.

Hypertension currently accounts for approximately 7 percent of all deaths worldwide, and this figure will no doubt increase as more societies adopt the habits and lifestyle of industrial nations. There is no returning to our evolutionary home-

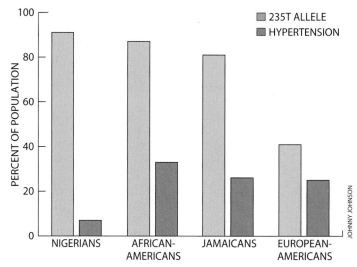

RATES OF A PARTICULAR GENE VARIANT—235T—and of hypertension in different ethnic groups yield a puzzling picture. Scientists expected that people who carried 235T would have a high incidence of hypertension. Yet that association has not held true universally. For instance, 235T is very common in Nigerians, in whom high blood pressure is rare. The findings suggest that a single gene cannot control the development of high blood pressure.

land, so science must lead us forward to another solution. The sanitary revolution was born of the awareness of contagion. Heart disease became a tractable problem when researchers recognized the importance of lifetime dietary habits on cholesterol metabolism. Prevention and treatment of hypertension will require a fuller appreciation of how genes and the environment join forces to disrupt blood pressure regulation.

We also believe that to understand hypertension in African-Americans better, the scientific community should reevaluate what the ethnic and racial divisions of our species mean. Many disciplines hold that there is no biological basis to the concept of race; instead they view it as a reflection of societal distinctions rather than readily defined scientific ones. Physical anthropologists, for instance, long ago ceased their attempts to classify *Homo sapiens* into various races, or subspecies. The disciplines of medicine and epidemiology, however, continue to ascribe biological meaning to racial designations, arguing that race is useful not only for distinguishing between groups of people but also for explaining the prevalence of certain disorders. Yet the racial classifications they incorporate in their studies are not based on rigorous scientific criteria but instead on bureaucratic categories, such as those used in the U.S. census.

As researchers grapple with the scientific import of race, its societal meaning must not be forgotten. We live in a world in which racial designations assume unfortunate significance. The destructive effects of racism complicate any study of how a disease such as hypertension affects minority groups. But as we continue to explore the complex interactions between external risk factors, such as stress and obesity, and the genes associated with the regulation of blood pressure, the results should offer guidance for all of us, regardless of skin color. **SA**

The Authors

RICHARD S. COOPER, CHARLES N. ROTIMI and RYK WARD have worked together on hypertension for eight years. Cooper received his medical degree from the University of Arkansas and completed training in clinical cardiology at Montefiore Hospital in Bronx, N.Y. He has written widely about the significance of race in biomedical research. Cooper and Rotimi are both at the Stritch School of Medicine at Loyola University Chicago. Rotimi studied biochemistry at the University of Benin in his native Nigeria before emigrating to the U.S. He serves as a consultant to the National Human Genome Research Institute and directs the field research program on diabetes and hypertension in Nigeria; the program is run by Loyola and the National Institutes of Health. Ward is professor and head of the Institute of Biological Anthropology at the University of Oxford. He was trained in New Zealand as an anthropologist and a human geneticist.

Further Reading

FAMILIAL AGGREGATION AND GENETIC EPIDEMIOLOGY OF BLOOD PRESSURE. Ryk Ward in *Hypertension: Pathophysiology, Diagnosis and Management.* Edited by J. H. Laragh and B. M. Brenner. Raven Press, 1990.
MOLECULAR BASIS OF HUMAN HYPERTENSION: ROLE OF ANGIOTENSINOGEN. X. Jeunemaitre, F. Soubrier, Y. V. Kotelevtsev, R. P. Lifton, C. S. Williams, A. Charu et al. in *Cell*, Vol. 71, No. 1, pages 169–180; October 1992.
THE SLAVERY HYPOTHESIS FOR HYPERTENSION AMONG AFRICAN AMERICANS: THE HISTORICAL EVIDENCE. Philip D. Curtin in *American Journal of Public Health*, Vol. 82, No. 12, pages 1681–1686; December 1992.
HYPERTENSION IN POPULATIONS OF WEST AFRICAN ORIGIN: IS THERE A GENETIC PREDISPOSITION? Richard S. Cooper and Charles N. Rotimi in *Journal of Hypertension*, Vol. 12, No. 3, pages 215–227; March 1994.
HYPERTENSION PREVALENCE IN SEVEN POPULATIONS OF AFRICAN ORIGIN. Richard S. Cooper, Charles N. Rotimi, Susan L. Ataman, Daniel L. McGee, Babatunde Osotimehin, Solomon Kadiri, Walinjom Muna, Samuel Kingue, Henry Fraser, Terrence Forrester, Franklyn Bennett and Rainford Wilks in *American Journal of Public Health*, Vol. 87, No. 2, pages 160–168; February 1997.

Negroes in the Bilge,
engraved by Deroi, circa 1835

NEGROES IN THE BILGE, ENGRAVED BY DEROI, PUBLISHED BY ENGELMANN, CIRCA 1835 (LITHO) BY JOHANN MORITZ RUGENDAS (1802–1858) Stapleton Collection, U.K./Bridgeman Art Library, London/New York

High Blood Pressure and the Slave Trade

One frequently cited—but controversial—explanation for the prevalence of chronic high blood pressure among U.S. blacks has to do with the voyage from Africa to America on slave ships, known as the Middle Passage. During such trips, the proposal goes, the slaves were placed in a Darwinian "survival-of-the-fittest" situation, in which staying alive depended on having the right genes—genes that now might confer an increased risk for high blood pressure.

Scientists often invoke evolutionary theory to account for why a certain racial or ethnic group appears to be at greater risk for a particular condition. The argument usually proceeds as follows: The population experienced a so-called selective pressure that favored the survival of some members of the group (and their genes) while eliminating others. If the remaining population did not mix genes with other racial or ethnic groups, certain genetic traits would begin to appear with increasing frequency. Assuming that African-Americans have a genetic predisposition to hypertension, evolutionary theorists ask, what was the unique, extreme selective pressure that led to this harmful trait becoming so common?

Some researchers suggest that the brutal voyage in slave ships was exactly this kind of event. Not surprisingly, slaves had extraordinarily high death rates before, during and after coming to American plantations. Many of the deaths were related to what doctors call salt-wasting conditions—diarrhea, dehydration and certain infections. Thus, the ability to retain salt might have had a survival value for the Africans brought to America. Under modern conditions, however, retaining salt would predispose the descendants of those people to hypertension.

Despite its immediate appeal, the slavery hypothesis is, in our view, quite problematic and has unfortunately been accepted uncritically. The historical framework for this hypothesis has been questioned by scholars of African history. For instance, there is no strong historical evidence that salt-wasting conditions were, in fact, the leading cause of death on slave ships. Africans on board these ships died for a variety of reasons, among them tuberculosis (not a salt-wasting infection) and violence.

The biological basis for the theory is also rather weak. Diarrhea and other salt-wasting diseases, particularly in children, have been among the most deadly killers for every population over humankind's entire evolutionary history. Any resulting selective pressures caused by such conditions would therefore apply to all racial and ethnic groups. And at least in the Caribbean during the 18th century, whites had little better survival rates than the slaves did—again indicating that any evolutionary pressure was not limited to Africans. Finally, current data suggest that Africans who have moved to Europe in the past several decades also have higher blood pressure than whites do, pointing to either environmental effects or something general in the African genetic background.

Researchers do not yet know enough about the genes for salt sensitivity to test the Middle Passage hypothesis directly. But some indirect evidence is informative. If the Middle Passage functioned as an evolutionary bottleneck, it should have reduced both the size of the population and the genetic variability within it, because only people with a very specific genetic makeup would survive. The data available, however, show a great deal of genetic diversity—not uniformity—among African-Americans.

The problem with the slavery hypothesis is that it provides a short-cut to a genetic and racial theory about why blacks have higher rates of hypertension. The responsive chord it strikes among scholars and the general public reflects a willingness to accept genetic explanations about the differences between whites and nonwhites without fully evaluating the evidence available. That attitude is obviously a significant obstacle to sound, unbiased research. As genetic research becomes more objective, with the ability to measure actual variations in DNA sequences, it might force society to abandon racial and ethnic prejudices, or it might offer them new legitimacy. Which outcome occurs will depend on how well scientists interpret the findings within a context that takes into account the complexities of society and history.   —R.S.C., C.N.R. and R.W.

The Placebo Effect

Colds, asthma, high blood pressure and heart disease are among the many conditions that can respond to treatment with a placebo.

Should doctors be prescribing sugar pills?

by Walter A. Brown

After a day of cross-country skiing in subfreezing weather a couple of years ago, I developed severe lower back pain. Even tying my shoes was agony. Despite my suffering, I knew there was no serious underlying disease, so I was certain I would be back to normal in no time.

But the days wore on with no change. A heating pad and suggestions from a friend with a chronic back problem (lie down, tuck your chin when you bend over) didn't help. After a week, I became desperate. I called my cousin Gary, who is a physical therapist. When I have consulted him in the past about sprains and tendonitis, his advice has always been on target. I was confident I was in the hands of an expert.

As usual, Gary was upbeat and authoritative. After taking my history and putting me through some maneuvers, he identified the muscles involved. He told me to ice the area, prescribed a set of exercises to stretch the constricted muscles and suggested that I take ibuprofen. When the consultation was over, I still had the back pain, but I had a technique for relieving it and the conviction that it would improve. Although my back was not yet better, I was.

I avoided the ibuprofen (it upsets my stomach), but I applied ice and exercised faithfully. Every time I did these things I felt a real sense of satisfaction. I was finally taking charge. Within two days the back pain had been reduced to a twinge; in a week it was gone.

I don't know whether the ice and exercise actually healed my inflamed, constricted muscles or whether they would have healed on their own in the same time. I do know that just seeking and receiving treatment made me feel better—less disabled, less distressed, more hopeful—and this in turn may have speeded my recovery. These benefits are called, often derisively, the placebo effect.

Powerful Healing

Medicine has become vastly more scientific in the past century—gone are the potions, brews and bloodlettings of antiquity. Nevertheless, doctors and their patients continue to ascribe healing powers to pills and procedures that have no intrinsic therapeutic value for the condition being treated (think of the widespread—and medically pointless—use of antibiotics to fight colds and flus caused by viruses). Some studies, including one by the U.S. Office of Technology Assessment, suggest that only about 20 percent of modern medical remedies in common use have been scientifically proved to be effective; the rest have not been subjected to empirical trials of whether or not

they work and, if so, how. It is not that these treatments do not offer benefits: most of them do. But in some cases, the benefit may come from the placebo effect, in which the very act of undergoing treatment—seeing a medical expert, for instance, or taking a pill—helps the patient to recover.

Since the early 1980s, I have been investigating the placebo effect. In the course of my research, I have learned something about how placebos work, why they are disparaged by both patients and physicians, and who is most likely to benefit from them. My information on these matters is far from complete. But based on what is known, I believe that the placebo effect is a powerful part of healing and that more effort should be made to harness and enhance it.

My interest in the placebo effect began when my colleagues and I found something unexpected while investigating the biochemistry of depression. In 1984 we were testing patients for the hormone cortisol, which is produced by the adrenal gland. In previous work, we and others had found that about half the patients with severe clinical depression produced excessive amounts of the hormone. We thought this group of patients might do better taking antidepressants than depressed patients with normal levels of cortisol would. (We speculated that patients with a biochemical imbalance might respond better to a biochemical treatment.)

To test this idea, we recorded levels of cortisol in patients who were about to enter a study of a new antidepressant medication. Mihály Arató, a young Hungarian psychiatrist working in my

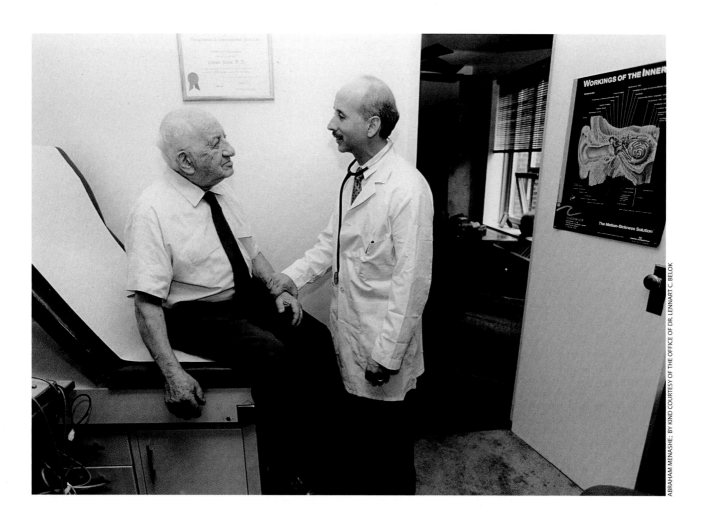

The healing environment
is a powerful antidote for illness.

The decision to seek medical assistance restores some sense of control.
The symbols and rituals of healing—the doctor's office, the stethoscope,
the physical examination—offer reassurance.

laboratory at the time, took on the job of analyzing the results. At first glance, the conclusions were disappointing. Contrary to our hypothesis, depressed patients responded equally well to the drug, regardless of how much hormone was present in their system. And yet they did show one fascinating difference.

This research was part of a so-called double-blind study: some patients were treated with a placebo, and neither the doctors nor the patients knew who received the placebo and who received the antidepressant. When Arató examined the results from the placebo group, the outcome was striking. Typically 30 to 40 percent of depressed patients benefit from taking a placebo. In this case, close to half the 22 patients with normal levels of cortisol felt better after taking a placebo, but among the nine patients with elevated levels, none improved.

These findings, which have been confirmed in our lab and by other researchers, indicate that depressed patients who respond to placebos differ biochemically from those who do not. I wondered if they differed in other ways as well. As it turns out, they do. People suffering from short-term depression, lasting less than three months, for instance, are more likely to benefit from a placebo. But longer-term depression, lasting more

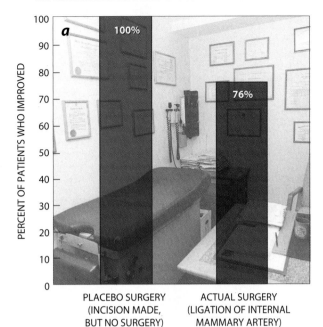

PERCENT OF PATIENTS WHO IMPROVED

a

100%

76%

PLACEBO SURGERY
(INCISION MADE,
BUT NO SURGERY)

ACTUAL SURGERY
(LIGATION OF INTERNAL
MAMMARY ARTERY)

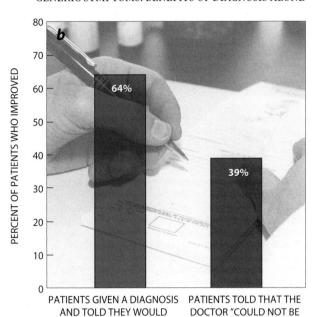

PERCENT OF PATIENTS WHO IMPROVED

b

64%

39%

PATIENTS GIVEN A DIAGNOSIS
AND TOLD THEY WOULD
BE BETTER IN A FEW DAYS

PATIENTS TOLD THAT THE
DOCTOR "COULD NOT BE
SURE WHAT WAS WRONG"

than a year or so, often does not improve after placebo treatment.

Relieving Stress

The placebo effect is not unique to depression or psychiatric illness. A landmark study in the early 1950s by Henry K. Beecher of Harvard University suggested that for a wide range of afflictions, including pain, high blood pressure, asthma and cough, roughly 30 to 40 percent of patients experience relief after taking a placebo. In some cases, the response can be even more pronounced: researchers led by Edmunds G. Dimond of the University of Kansas Medical Center in the late 1950s investigated the effectiveness of the then routine arterial ligation surgery to treat angina pectoris (chest pain caused by insufficient blood supply to the heart). The doctors performed the surgical procedure in one set of 13 patients; with a second group of five patients, they made only a chest incision but did no further surgery. Among the patients who received the actual surgery, 76 percent improved. Notably, 100 percent of the placebo group got better. (Arterial ligation surgery is no longer performed.)

So what exactly is this placebo treatment that compares so favorably with conventional methods? Placebos are usually defined not in terms of what they are but what

they are not. They are often described as inactive, but placebo agents are clearly active: they exert influence and can be quite effective in eliciting beneficial responses. Placebos are also described as nonspecific, presumably because they relieve multiple conditions and because exactly how they work is not fully understood. Yet by either of these standards, placebos are no less specific than many valid and accepted remedies, such as aspirin or certain tranquilizers. Most narrowly, a placebo is a pharmacologically inert capsule or injection,

yet even this definition does not capture the full range of procedures that can have a placebo effect.

Today the most common situation in which people use substances known to be placebos is during double-blind clinical trials. Patients who take a placebo in the course of such trials receive much more than a pharmacologically inert substance: like the patients receiving a "real" drug, they benefit from a thorough medical evaluation, a chance to discuss their condition, a diagnosis and a plausible treatment plan. Patients also

---

Medicine has become vastly more scientific
in the past century—gone are the potions,
brews and bloodlettings of antiquity.

Nevertheless, doctors and their patients
continue to ascribe healing powers
to pills and procedures
that have no intrinsic therapeutic value.

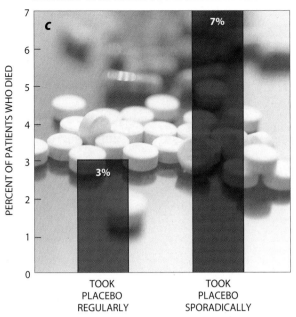

MYOCARDIAL INFARCTION: BENEFITS OF ADHERING TO TREATMENT ROUTINE

c

PERCENT OF PATIENTS WHO DIED

7 —
6 —
5 —
4 —
3 — **3%**
2 —
1 —
0 —

TOOK PLACEBO REGULARLY — TOOK PLACEBO SPORADICALLY **7%**

ABRAHAM MENASHE (*photographs*); JENNIFER C. CHRISTIANSEN (*graphs*); SOURCES: (*a*) E. G. DIMOND ET AL., 1960; (*b*) K. B. THOMAS, 1987; (*c*) R. I. HORWITZ, 1990

The placebo effect is not unique to psychiatric illness.

For a wide range of afflictions, 30 to 40 percent of patients experience relief after taking a placebo.

PLACEBOS ARE EFFECTIVE for a variety of conditions. Patients with angina pectoris (insufficient blood flow to the heart) responded to placebo surgery in which doctors made only an incision in the chest but did nothing further (*a*). In a study of patients with generic symptoms but no organic ailment, researchers found that reassuring words from a doctor helped patients to feel better (*b*). And in a study of the drug propranolol, which is used after heart attacks to prevent further damage, investigators noticed that patients who took placebo pills regularly had a lower death rate than patients who took placebos sporadically (*c*).

typically enjoy the enthusiasm, effort, commitment and respect of their doctors and nurses. These factors, which many people view as incidental to the healing process, provide an important clue as to why placebos work.

The healing environment is a powerful antidote for illness. The decision to seek medical assistance restores some sense of control. The symbols and rituals of healing—the doctor's office, the stethoscope, the physical examination—offer reassurance. An explanation for the illness and a prognosis, when favorable, reduce fear; even when the report is unfavorable, it allays the anxiety of uncertainty. And merely the act of taking a pill can have a therapeutic effect. For example, the drug propranolol is often prescribed after a heart attack to regulate the heartbeat and prevent further damage. In a recent study of more than 2,000 patients, the death rate was cut in half among patients who took propranolol regularly compared with those who took the medication less regularly. But in the same study, patients who took placebos regularly also had half the death rate of those who took them less regularly—even though the two groups of placebo users were similar medically and psychologically.

Notably, placebos seem to be most reliably effective for afflictions in which stress directly affects the symptoms: in certain forms of depression and anxiety, for example, distress *is* the illness. And conditions such as pain, asthma and

moderate high blood pressure can become worse when the patient is upset. Indeed, placebos may work in part by lessening the apprehension associated with disease. Studies of both animals and humans have shown that the functioning of the immune system falters under stressful conditions. For instance, stress increases the secretion of hormones such as cortisol, which in turn lowers resistance to disease. It is not inconceivable that by reducing anxiety, placebos could influence countless diseases, including some that we do not usually think of as subject to psychological influence.

Great Expectations

A patient's expectation of improvement is also crucial. Researchers know that across a wide range of illnesses, patients who think they will feel better are more likely to do so. Expectation operates more specifically as well. For example, when participants in a study were told that their pharmacologically inert drink contained alcohol, they often felt and acted intoxicated and even showed some of the physiological signs of intoxication. A 1968 study led by Thomas J. Luparello of the State University of New York Downstate Medical Center in Brooklyn showed that patients with asthma who were given an inhaler containing only nebulized saltwater but were told they would be inhaling an irritant or allergen displayed

more problems with airway obstruction. When the same group was told that the inhaler had a medicine to help asthma, their airways opened up.

Given their demonstrated effectiveness, why do placebos have such a dubious reputation? The word "placebo" itself comes with unfortunate baggage. Latin for "I shall please," it is the first word of the vespers for the dead, and in the 12th century these vespers were commonly referred to as placebos. By the 1300s, the term had become secular and pejorative, suggesting a flatterer or sycophant, a meaning probably derived from the depreciation of professional mourners, those paid to sing placebos. When the word entered medical terminology, the negative connotation stuck. It was defined as a medicine given to please patients rather than to benefit them. In the modern era, the lack of pharmacological activity became part of the definition as well.

As a result, the name brings with it connotations of deception and inauthenticity. A modern myth about placebos reflects this stigma: if a condition improves with placebos, the condition is supposedly "all in the head." But the many examples of physical ailments—high blood pressure, angina pectoris and asthma, to name a few—that respond to placebos demonstrate that this notion is far from the case.

The very effectiveness of a placebo is troublesome to us doctors and to other medical experts. It impugns the value of our most cherished remedies, it hampers the development of new therapeutics, and it threatens our livelihood. Nevertheless, given the astounding advances in medical technology over the past two decades, including the development of indisputably efficacious drugs and procedures, we in the medical community may now be ready—secure that medicine is scientific—to accept and put to good use this component of healing that we do not fully understand.

Decades of research offer guidance as to how physicians can incorporate aspects of the placebo effect, in ways that are both medically and ethically sound, to make accepted medicines more effective. Yet many of these ideas have not been tried by doctors. Some of the suggestions are not surprising. For instance, patients should be made to feel confident and secure that they are in the hands of a recognized healer; diplomas, board certifications and medical instruments in sight generally provide these signals. Patients should also be reassured by items associated with the relief of symptoms—a white coat, a physical examination, a written prescription when necessary. A careful analysis of a patient's complaint is far more comforting than an immediate diagnosis, no matter how accurate.

Administering a thorough evaluation, however, does not mean that a patient should be subjected to unnecessary diagnostic procedures. Rather the doctor should listen carefully, ask suitable questions and perform a complete examination. The fact that someone has bronchitis may be obvious to a doctor within seconds; an additional five minutes of evaluation that includes a stethoscope on the chest may not add to the accuracy of the diagnosis, but it does add to the patient's confidence. Physicians and nurses of yesterday seemed to understand intuitively the importance of a good bedside manner. Many of today's medical experts still appreciate the healing power of a compassionate consultation, but under pressure to provide "cost-effective" care, they (and particularly insurance companies) may be losing sight of this crucial component of effective care.

The initial evaluation should include

If physicians can see placebos as broadly effective therapies,

whose mechanisms of action are not completely understood and which tend to be more effective for some conditions than others,

they can then offer placebos both honestly and as plausible treatment.

specific questions regarding the patient's previous experiences with a variety of remedies, including treatments (such as alternative therapies) most physicians consider to be placebos. What has worked and what has not for this person? In particular, the doctor or nurse should elicit the patient's ideas about what might or might not be helpful for the present complaint.

Determining a Diagnosis

The physician should provide a diagnosis and a prognosis whenever possible. In a recent study of 200 patients with physical complaints but no identifiable disease, doctors at the University of Southampton in England told some that no serious disease had been found and that they would soon be well; others heard that the cause of their ailment was unclear. Two weeks later 64 percent of the first group had recovered, but only 39 percent of the second group had recuperated.

If a specific drug or medical procedure is called for, it should be offered with realistic optimism and information about its specific desirable effects—something along the lines of "This medicine will help you breathe" for an asthma medication. The doctor should also provide information about side effects and about the most likely course of symptoms. This information adds to the patient's confidence and to the sense that the condition is known and controllable.

If a number of treatment options are equally appropriate, the patient should be given the chance to make a choice.

But doctors should offer a limited number of options (no more than three or four) and should provide sound information to help the patient in making the decision. Allowing patients—no matter how well informed they may be—to choose whatever course of therapy they would like deprives them of a major benefit of seeking medical advice. If people want to treat themselves, and many do, they do not go to experts.

When managing conditions such as the common cold that typically run their course without treatment or when handling diseases such as certain cancers that have no effective treatment, doctors often prescribe palliative medication to relieve symptoms such as congestion or pain. For these therapies to be most useful, however, it is important that doctors offer them with the same thoughtfulness and authority as when they recommend other, more definitive remedies.

In practice, though, this is not always the case. Doctors often tell patients with colds or the flu that they will probably feel better in a few days and that they can take cold medicine if they want to. Such patients, feeling miserable and bereft of treatment, often request and receive antibiotics—pharmacologically active but inappropriate drugs that they are unwittingly using as placebos. These same patients would very likely feel quite differently if, after a medical examination complete with diagnostic instruments, their doctors wrote the name of a cold medicine on a prescription form (even if the drug did not require a prescription) and handed it to them with instructions on how and over what interval this medicine will be helpful.

Some of these suggestions may seem like hocus-pocus. Yet I see them as an approach to medicine informed by an understanding of all the processes involved in healing. In the case of the common cold, such an approach could go a long way toward reducing the unnecessary use of antibiotics and the attendant expense and dangers of the practice.

Prescribing Placebos

What about the deliberate use of placebos? Should physicians, in order to take advantage of the placebo effect, prescribe drugs or procedures that they know to be of no intrinsic value?

For many medical experts, this situation presents what has seemed an insolvable dilemma. Doctors have felt that if they tell patients they are prescribing a sugar pill, the placebo response, which depends in part on patients' expectations of receiving a plausible remedy, will be lost. On the other hand, if doctors tell patients that the placebo is a pharmacologically active medicine, they are engaging in a type of deception that is neither ethical nor, in the long run, therapeutic. I think much of this dilemma arises from the pejorative connotations

ABRAHAM MENASHE

associated with placebos and a general uncertainty about their value.

If physicians can see placebos—like many conventional drugs—as broadly effective therapies, whose mechanisms of action are not completely understood and which tend to be more effective for some conditions than others, they can then offer placebos both honestly and as plausible treatment. The decision to prescribe a placebo should be based, as with any drug, on the risks and benefits. The specific placebo chosen should be free of toxicity and should be in keeping with the patient's beliefs and expectations. In this regard, it is worth noting that, according to a study published in 1993 in the *New England Journal of Medicine,* at least 30 percent of adult Americans use alternative medicine—such as massage, homeopathy, spiritual healing and megavitamins—and that the total number of visits to alternative therapy providers each year exceeds the number of visits to primary care physicians. Although alternative medicine healers and their patients believe fervently in the effectiveness of megavitamins and herbal mixtures, many of these popular remedies probably derive their benefit from the placebo effect.

So how can a doctor ethically prescribe a placebo? Consider a specific example—the treatment of mild to moderately high blood pressure. Clinical trials, such as the study conducted in the early 1990s by Barry J. Materson of the Veterans Affairs Medical Center in Miami, have shown that at least 20 percent of people with this condition achieve normal blood pressure after several weeks of taking placebos. Because blood pressure medication is expensive and has troublesome side effects, some patients might want to consider taking a placebo as a course of treatment.

A doctor could explain the situation to a patient in the following manner: "You have several options. One is to take a diuretic. It will probably bring your blood pressure down, but it does have some side effects. There are also other treatments that are less expensive and less likely to cause side effects and that help many people with your condition. Some find that herbal tea twice a day is helpful; others find that taking these pills twice a day is helpful. These pills do not contain any drug. We do not know how the herbal tea or these pills work. They may trigger or stimulate your body's own healing processes. We do know that about 20 percent of the people with your type of high blood pressure get their blood pressure into the normal range using this approach. If you decide to try one of these treatments, I will check your progress every two weeks. If after six weeks your blood pressure is still high, we should consider the diuretic."

Disease is typically defined as an abnormal state of the body—high blood glucose, a fractured forearm, a lung infection. But illness is something else: it is the suffering that accompanies disease. In our culture, pills and other symbols of the physician's healing arts have great power to ease that suffering. As physicians, we should respect the benefits of placebos—their safety, effectiveness and low cost—and bring the full advantage of these benefits into our everyday practices. [SA]

The Author

WALTER A. BROWN has been with the psychiatry department at the Brown University School of Medicine since 1974. About 10 years ago he established a research center in Rhode Island to carry out clinical trials of psychiatric drugs. He is currently working on a study of brain function and measures of immunity during experimentally induced emotion. Brown is a fellow of the American Psychiatric Association and a member of the American College of Neuropsychopharmacology.

Further Reading

PERSUASION AND HEALING. Jerome D. Frank and Julia B. Frank. Johns Hopkins University Press, 1991.
HARNESSING PLACEBO EFFECTS IN HEALTH CARE. D. Mark Chaput de Saintonge and Andrew Herxheimer in *Lancet,* Vol. 344, No. 8928, pages 995–998; October 8, 1994.
THE PLACEBO EFFECT: AN INTERDISCIPLINARY EXPLORATION. Edited by Anne Harrington. Harvard University Press, 1997.

Dying to Be Thin

Eating disorders cripple—literally—millions of young women, in large part because treatments are not always effective or accessible

by Kristin Leutwyler,
staff writer

I don't own a scale. I don't trust myself to have one in the house—maybe in the same way that recovered alcoholics rightfully clear their cabinets of cold medicines and mouthwash. At 5'7", I know that I usually weigh 118 pounds, and I know that is considered normal for my frame. But 13 years ago, when I was 15 years old and the same height, I weighed 67 pounds, and I thought I was grossly, repulsively obese.

My own bout with anorexia nervosa—the eating disorder that made me starve myself into malnutrition—was severe but short-lived. I had a wonderful physician who worked hard to earn my trust and safeguard my health. And I had one great friend who slowly, over many months, proved to me that one ice cream cone wouldn't make me fat nor would being fat make me unlovable. A year later I was back up to 95 pounds. I was still scrawny, but at least I knew it.

I was—am—lucky. Eating disorders are often chronic and startlingly common. One percent of all teenage girls suffer from anorexia nervosa at some point. Two to 3 percent develop bulimia nervosa, a condition in which sufferers consume large amounts of food only to then "purge" away the excess calories by making themselves vomit, by abusing laxatives and diuretics, or by exercising obsessively. And binge eaters—who overeat until they are uncomfortably full—make up another 2 percent of the population.

In addition to the mental pain these illnesses cause sufferers and their families and friends, they also have devastating physical consequences. In the most serious cases, binge eating can rupture the stomach or esophagus. Purging can flush the body of vital minerals, causing cardiac arrest. Self-starvation can also lead to heart failure. Among anorexics, who undergo by far the worst complications, the mortality rate after 10 years is 7.7 percent, reports Katherine A. Halmi, a professor of psychiatry at Cornell University and director of the Eating Disorders Clinic at New York Hospital in Westchester. After 30 years of struggling with the condition, one fifth die.

Because studies clearly show that people who recover sooner are less likely to relapse, the push continues to discover better treatments. Eating disorders are exceedingly complex diseases, brought on by a mix of environmental, social and biological factors. But in recent years, scientists have made some small advances. Various forms of therapy are proving beneficial, and some medications—particularly a class of antidepressants known as selective serotonin reuptake inhibitors (SSRIs)—are helping certain patients. "SSRIs are not wonder drugs for eating disorders," says Robert I. Berkowitz of the University of Pennsylvania. "But treatments have become more successful, and so we're feeling hopeful, even though we have a long way to go to understand these diseases."

Weighing the Risks

When I began working on this article, I phoned my former physician, a specialist in adolescent medicine, and I was a little surprised that she remembered my name but not my diagnosis. In all fairness, my illness was a textbook case. I had faced many common risk factors, starting with a "fat list" on the bulletin board at my ballet school. The list named girls who needed to lose weight and by how much. I was never on it. But the possibility filled me with so much dread that at the

Anorexia nervosa affects many young women, such as this patient in the eating disorders clinic at the New York State Psychiatric Institute, a part of Columbia-Presbyterian Medical Center.

start of the summer, I decided I had to get into better shape. I did sit-ups and ran every day before and after ballet classes. I stopped eating sweets, fats and meat. And when I turned 15 in September, I was as lean and strong as I've ever been.

Scientists know that environment contributes heavily to the development of eating disorders. Many anorexic and bulimic women are involved in ballet, modeling or some other activity that values low body weight. Men with eating disorders often practice sports that emphasize dieting and fasting, such as wrestling and track. And waiflike figures in fashion and the media clearly hold considerable sway. "The cultural ideal for beauty for women has become increasingly thin over the years," Berkowitz notes. In keeping, among the millions now affected by eating disorders every year, more than 90 percent are female.

Like me, most young women first de-velop an eating disorder as they near puberty. "Girls start to plump up at puberty," Estherann M. Grace of Children's Hospital in Boston says. "And this is also when they start looking at magazines and thinking, 'What's wrong with me?'" Recognizing that anorexia nervosa often arises as girls begin to mature physically, psychiatrists recently revised the diagnostic standards. "It used to be that one of the criteria was that you had to have missed a period or suffered from amenorrhea for three months," says Marcie B. Schneider of North Shore University Hospital. "And so we missed all those kids with eating disorders who had not yet reached puberty or had delayed it." Now the criteria include a failure to meet expected growth stages, and more 10-, 11- and 12-year-olds are being diagnosed.

Puberty is a stressful time—and stressful events typically precede the onset of psychiatric conditions, including eating disorders. Maybe I would have stopped dieting had my parents not separated in the summer, or my grandmother had not died that fall, or I hadn't spent my entire winter vacation dancing 30-odd performances of the *Nutcracker*. Maybe. I do know that as my life spun out of control around me, my diet became the one thing I felt I could still rein in. "Anorexics are terribly fearful of a loss of control," Grace says, "and eating gives them one area in which they feel they have it."

Most people under stress will overeat or undereat, Grace adds, but biology and personality types make some more vulnerable to extremes. Anorexics tend to be good students, dedicated athletes and perfectionists—and so it makes some sense that in dieting, too, they are highly disciplined. In contrast, bulimics and binge eaters are typically outgoing and adventurous, prone to impulsive behaviors. And all three illnesses frequently arise in conjunction with depression, anxiety and obsessive-compulsive disorder—conditions that tend to run in families and are related to malfunctions in the system regulating the neurotransmitter serotonin.

I most definitely became obsessed. I read gourmet magazines cover to cover, trying to imagine the taste of foods I would not let myself have—ever. I cut my calories back to 800 a day. I counted them down to the singles in a diet soda. I measured and weighed my food to make my tally more accurate. And I ate everything I dished, to make sure I knew the precise number of calories I had eaten. By November, none of my clothes fit. When I sat, I got bruises where my hip bones jutted out in the back. My hair thinned, and my nails became brittle. I was continuously exhausted, incredibly depressed and had no intention of quitting. It felt like a success.

Sitting Down for Treatment

The first barrier to treating eating disorders is getting people to admit that they have one. Because bulimics are often a normal weight and hide their strange eating rituals, they can be very hard to identify. Similarly, binge eaters are extremely secretive about their practices. And even though seriously ill anorexics are quite noticeably emaciated, they are the least willing of all patients with eating disorders to get help. "Anorectics are not motivated for treatment in the same way as bulimics are," Halmi comments. "Because anorexia gives patients a sense

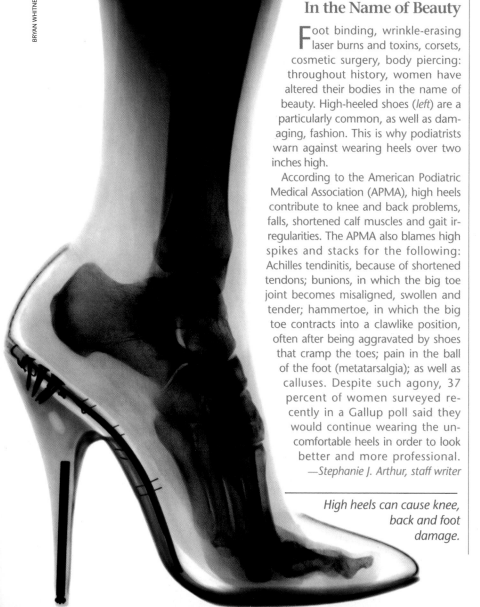

BRYAN WHITNEY

In the Name of Beauty

Foot binding, wrinkle-erasing laser burns and toxins, corsets, cosmetic surgery, body piercing: throughout history, women have altered their bodies in the name of beauty. High-heeled shoes (*left*) are a particularly common, as well as damaging, fashion. This is why podiatrists warn against wearing heels over two inches high.

According to the American Podiatric Medical Association (APMA), high heels contribute to knee and back problems, falls, shortened calf muscles and gait irregularities. The APMA also blames high spikes and stacks for the following: Achilles tendinitis, because of shortened tendons; bunions, in which the big toe joint becomes misaligned, swollen and tender; hammertoe, in which the big toe contracts into a clawlike position, often after being aggravated by shoes that cramp the toes; pain in the ball of the foot (metatarsalgia); as well as calluses. Despite such agony, 37 percent of women surveyed recently in a Gallup poll said they would continue wearing the uncomfortable heels in order to look better and more professional.
—*Stephanie J. Arthur, staff writer*

High heels can cause knee, back and foot damage.

of control, it is seen as a positive thing in their lives, and they're terrified to give that up."

I certainly was—and a large part of getting better involved changing that way of thinking. To that end, cognitive behavioral therapy (CBT) has had fair success in treating people with anorexia, bulimia and binge eating disorder. "There are three main components," explains Halmi, who views CBT as one of the most effective treatments. Patients keep diaries of what they eat, how they feel when they eat and what events, if any, prompt them to eat. I used to feel guilty before meals and would ask my mother for permission before I ate. She never would have denied me, but asking somehow lessened my guilt.

CBT also helps patients identify flawed perceptions (such as thinking they are fat) and, with the aid of a therapist, list evidence for and against these ideas and then try to correct them. This process let me eventually see the lack of reason in my belief that, say, a single cookie would lure me into a lifetime bender of reckless eating and obesity. And CBT patients work through strategies for handling situations that reinforce their abnormal perceptions. I got rid of my scale and avoided mirrors.

Working in collaboration with researchers at Stanford University, the University of Minnesota and the University of North Dakota, Halmi is now comparing relapse rates in anorexics who have been randomly assigned to treatment with CBT or the SSRI drug Prozac, or a combination of both. Unfortunately, the dropout rate has been high. But earlier evidence has suggested that Prozac—which had not yet been approved when I was sick—may benefit some patients, helping them to at least stop losing weight. "Essentially every young woman with anorexia is also dealing with depression, and so SSRIs help alleviate some of the somatic symptoms associated with that," Grace says.

Not everyone believes SSRIs do much for anorexics, particularly those who are not desperately ill. But SSRIs have proved effective in people with bulimia. In conjunction with James Mitchell, director of neuroscience at the University of North Dakota, and Scott J. Crow, professor of psychiatry at the University of Minnesota, Halmi has just completed collecting data on 100 bulimics who received cognitive behavioral therapy for four months. Those who still did not improve underwent further therapy and

drug treatment with Prozac. "When it comes to bulimia," Berkowitz tells me, "it is clear that both psychotherapy and pharmacology are helpful."

Swallowing the Truth

New treatments for eating disorders could benefit millions of adolescents—if they can get them. Most face a greater challenge getting help today than I did 13 years ago. "One of the big topics now is how to survive in this era of managed care," Schneider tells me. "You have to be at death's door to get into a psychiatric hospital," Berkowitz says, "and once a patient is stabilized, the reimbursements often stop. This is not an inexpensive disease to have." I went through a year of weekly therapy before I reached a stable, if not wholly healthy, weight. In comparison, Berkowitz notes that the insurance policies he has encountered recently often pay for only 20 sessions, with the patient responsible for a 50 percent co-payment.

"It's absolutely sinful," Halmi says. "It is a disaster for eating-disorder patients, particularly anorexics." She points out that relapse rates are much lower in adolescents who receive treatment long enough to get back up to 90 percent of their ideal weight; those who gain less typically fare worse. But insurance rarely lasts long enough. "It used to be you could hospitalize a kid for three or four months," Schneider says. "Now you can at most get a month or so, and it's on a case-by-case basis. You're fighting with the insurance company every three days." The fact that it may be cheaper to treat these patients right the first time seems to make little difference to insurance companies, she adds: "Their attitude is that these kids will probably have a different carrier down the road."

Down the road, the consequences of inadequate treatment are chilling. Debra K. Katzman of the Hospital for Sick Children in Toronto recently took magnetic resonance imaging (MRI) scans of young women with anorexia nervosa before and after recovery and found that the volume of cerebral gray matter in their brains seemed to have decreased—permanently. "The health of these kids does rapidly improve when they gain back some weight," Schneider says, "but the changes on the MRIs do not appear to go away."

In addition, those who do not receive sufficient nutrition during their teen years seriously damage their skeletal growth. "The bones are completed in the

second decade, right when this disease hits, so it sets people up for long-term problems," Grace asserts. These problems range from frequent fractures to thinning bones and premature osteoporosis. "I talked to one girl today who is 16. She hasn't been underweight for that long, but already she is lacking 25 percent of the bone density normal for kids her age," Schneider says. "And I have to explain to her why she has to do what no inch in her wants to—eat—so that she won't be in a wheelchair at age 50."

Because drugs used to treat bone loss in adults do nothing in teens, researchers are looking for ways to remedy this particular symptom. "[Loss of bone is] related to their not menstruating and not having estrogen," Grace explains. "But whereas estrogen does protect older women against bone loss, it doesn't seem to help younger ones." She and a coworker are now testing the protective effects of another hormone in young girls. Halmi also emphasizes that estrogen treatment for patients with eating disorders is a waste of time. Instead "you want to get them back up to a normal weight," she states, "and let the body start building bone itself."

All of which brings us back to the concept of normal weight—something many women simply don't want to be. A recent study found that even centerfold models felt the need to lie about their heights and weights. Christopher P. Szabo of the Tara Hospital in Johannesburg reviewed the reported measurements of women in South African editions of *Playboy* between February 1994 and February 1995 and calculated their apparent body mass indices. Even though these models all looked healthy, 72 percent had claimed heights and weights that gave them a body mass index below 18—the medical cutoff for malnourishment. "Maybe 5 percent of the population could achieve an 'ideal' figure, with surgical help," Grace jokes. "I'm sorry, but Barbie couldn't stand upright if she weren't plastic."

I remember all too well thinking that I would look fat at a normal weight. Sometimes I still do worry that I look fat. But I take my perceptions with a grain of salt. After all, I haven't exactly proved myself to be a good judge in that regard. Somehow I've come to a point where I don't need to measure my self-worth in pounds—or the lack thereof—provided I'm happy and well. I gave up a lot—ballet, friendships, a sense of community and security. But in return, I got my health back. ◼

Creating False Memories

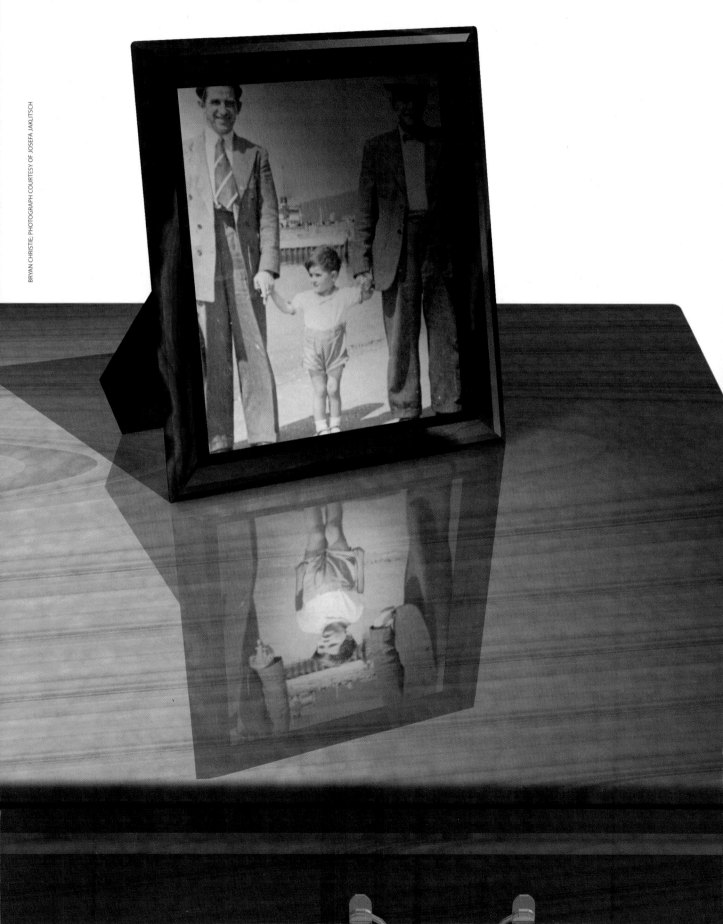

Researchers are showing how suggestion and imagination can create "memories" of events that did not actually occur

by Elizabeth F. Loftus

In 1986 Nadean Cool, a nurse's aide in Wisconsin, sought therapy from a psychiatrist to help her cope with her reaction to a traumatic event experienced by her daughter. During therapy, the psychiatrist used hypnosis and other suggestive techniques to dig out buried memories of abuse that Cool herself had allegedly experienced. In the process, Cool became convinced that she had repressed memories of having been in a satanic cult, of eating babies, of being raped, of having sex with animals and of being forced to watch the murder of her eight-year-old friend. She came to believe that she had more than 120 personalities—children, adults, angels and even a duck—all because, Cool was told, she had experienced severe childhood sexual and physical abuse. The psychiatrist also performed exorcisms on her, one of which lasted for five hours and included the sprinkling of holy water and screams for Satan to leave Cool's body.

When Cool finally realized that false memories had been planted, she sued the psychiatrist for malpractice. In March 1997, after five weeks of trial, her case was settled out of court for $2.4 million.

Nadean Cool is not the only patient to develop false memories as a result of questionable therapy. In Missouri in 1992 a church counselor helped Beth Rutherford to remember during therapy that her father, a clergyman, had regularly raped her between the ages of seven and 14 and that her mother sometimes helped him by holding her down. Under her therapist's guidance, Rutherford developed memories of her father twice impregnating her and forcing her to abort the fetus herself with a coat hanger. The father

had to resign from his post as a clergyman when the allegations were made public. Later medical examination of the daughter revealed, however, that she was still a virgin at age 22 and had never been pregnant. The daughter sued the therapist and received a $1-million settlement in 1996.

About a year earlier two juries returned verdicts against a Minnesota psychiatrist accused of planting false memories by former patients Vynnette Hamanne and Elizabeth Carlson, who under hypnosis and sodium amytal, and after being fed misinformation about the workings of memory, had come to remember horrific abuse by family members. The juries awarded Hammane $2.67 million and Carlson $2.5 million for their ordeals.

In all four cases, the women developed memories about childhood abuse in therapy and then later denied their authenticity. How can we determine if memories of childhood abuse are true or false? Without corroboration, it is very difficult to differentiate between false memories and true ones. Also, in these cases, some memories were contrary to physical evidence, such as explicit and detailed recollections of rape and abortion when medical examination confirmed virginity. How is it possible for people to acquire elaborate and confident false memories? A growing number of investigations demonstrate that under the right circumstances false memories can be instilled rather easily in some people.

My own research into memory distortion goes back to the early 1970s, when I began studies of the "misinformation effect." These studies show that when people who witness an event are later exposed to new and misleading information about it, their recollections often become distorted. In one example, participants viewed a simulated automobile accident at an intersection with

a stop sign. After the viewing, half the participants received a suggestion that the traffic sign was a yield sign. When asked later what traffic sign they remembered seeing at the intersection, those who had been given the suggestion tended to claim that they had seen a yield sign. Those who had not received the phony information were much more accurate in their recollection of the traffic sign.

My students and I have now conducted more than 200 experiments involving over 20,000 individuals that document how exposure to misinformation induces memory distortion. In these studies, people "recalled" a conspicuous barn in a bucolic scene that contained no buildings at all, broken glass and tape recorders that were not in the scenes they viewed, a white instead of a blue vehicle in a crime scene, and Minnie Mouse when they actually saw Mickey Mouse. Taken together, these studies show that misinformation can change an individual's recollection in predictable and sometimes very powerful ways.

Misinformation has the potential for invading our memories when we talk to other people, when we are suggestively interrogated or when we read or view media coverage about some event that we may have experienced ourselves. After more than two decades of exploring the power of misinformation, researchers have learned a great deal about the conditions that make people susceptible to memory modification. Memories are more easily modified, for instance, when the passage of time allows the original memory to fade.

False Childhood Memories

It is one thing to change a detail or two in an otherwise intact memory but quite another to plant a false memory of an event that never happened. To study false memory, my students and I

FALSE MEMORIES are often created by combining actual memories with suggestions received from others. The memory of a happy childhood outing to the beach with father and grandfather, for instance, can be distorted by a suggestion, perhaps from a relative, into a memory of being afraid or lost. False memories also can be induced when a person is encouraged to imagine experiencing specific events without worrying about whether they really happened or not.

first had to find a way to plant a pseudo-memory that would not cause our subjects undue emotional stress, either in the process of creating the false memory or when we revealed that they had been intentionally deceived. Yet we wanted to try to plant a memory that would be at least mildly traumatic, had the experience actually happened.

My research associate, Jacqueline E. Pickrell, and I settled on trying to plant a specific memory of being lost in a shopping mall or large department store at about the age of five. Here's how we did it. We asked our subjects, 24 individuals ranging in age from 18 to 53, to try to remember childhood events that had been recounted to us by a parent, an older sibling or another close relative. We prepared a booklet for each participant containing one-paragraph stories about three events that had actually happened to him or her and one that had not. We constructed the false event using information about a plausible shopping trip provided by a relative, who also verified that the participant had not in fact been lost at about the age of five. The lost-in-the-mall scenario included the following elements: lost for an extended period, crying, aid and comfort by an elderly woman and, finally, reunion with the family.

After reading each story in the book-let, the participants wrote what they remembered about the event. If they did not remember it, they were instructed to write, "I do not remember this." In two follow-up interviews, we told the participants that we were interested in examining how much detail they could remember and how their memories compared with those of their relative. The event paragraphs were not read to them verbatim, but rather parts were provided as retrieval cues. The participants recalled something about 49 of the 72 true events (68 percent) immediately after the initial reading of the booklet and also in each of the two follow-up interviews. After reading the booklet, seven of the 24 participants (29 percent) remembered either partially or fully the false event constructed for them, and in the two follow-up interviews six participants (25 percent) continued to claim that they remembered the fictitious event. Statistically, there were some differences between the true memories and the false ones: participants used more words to describe the true memories, and they rated the true memories as being somewhat more clear. But if an onlooker

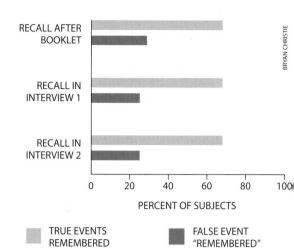

BRYAN CHRISTIE

were to observe many of our participants describe an event, it would be difficult indeed to tell whether the account was of a true or a false memory.

Of course, being lost, however frightening, is not the same as being abused. But the lost-in-the-mall study is not about real experiences of being lost; it is about planting false memories of being lost. The paradigm shows a way of instilling false memories and takes a step toward allowing us to understand how this might happen in real-world settings. Moreover, the study provides evidence that people can be led to remember their past in different ways, and they can

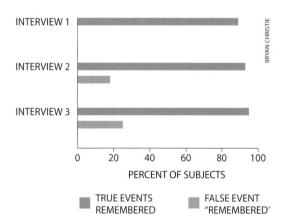

BRYAN CHRISTIE

RECALL OF PLANTED CHILDHOOD EVENTS in this study appears to increase slightly after the details become familiar to the subject and the source of the information is forgotten. Ira Hyman and his colleagues at Western Washington University presented subjects with true events provided by relatives along with a false event—such as spilling a punch bowl on the parents of the bride at a wedding. None of the participants remembered the false event when first told about it, but in two follow-up interviews, initially 18 percent and later 25 percent of the subjects said they remembered something about the incident.

Creating False Memories

FALSE MEMORY TOOK ROOT in roughly 25 percent of the subjects in this study by the author and her co-workers. The study was designed to create a false recollection of being lost at age five on a shopping trip. A booklet prepared for each participant included the false event and three events that he or she had actually experienced. After reading the scenarios, 29 percent of the subjects "recalled" something about being lost in the mall. Follow-up interviews showed there was little variation over time in recalling both the false and true events.

even be coaxed into "remembering" entire events that never happened.

Studies in other laboratories using a similar experimental procedure have produced similar results. For instance, Ira Hyman, Troy H. Husband and F. James Billing of Western Washington University asked college students to recall childhood experiences that had been recounted by their parents. The researchers told the students that the study was about how people remember shared experiences differently. In addition to actual events reported by parents, each participant was given one false event—either an overnight hospitalization for a high fever and a possible ear infection, or a birthday party with pizza and a clown—that supposedly happened at about the age of five. The parents confirmed that neither of these events actually took place.

Hyman found that students fully or partially recalled 84 percent of the true events in the first interview and 88 percent in the second interview. None of the participants recalled the false event during the first interview, but 20 percent said they remembered something about the false event in the second interview. One participant who had been exposed to the emergency hospitalization story later remembered a male doctor, a female nurse and a friend from church who came to visit at the hospital.

In another study, along with true events Hyman presented different false events, such as accidentally spilling a bowl of punch on the parents of the bride at a wedding reception or having to evacuate a grocery store when the overhead sprinkler systems erroneously activated. Again, none of the participants recalled the false event during the first interview, but 18 percent remembered something about it in the second interview and 25 percent in the third interview. For example, during the first interview, one participant, when asked about the fictitious wedding event, stated, "I have no clue. I have never heard that one before." In the second interview, the participant said, "It was an outdoor wedding, and I think we were

running around and knocked something over like the punch bowl or something and made a big mess and of course got yelled at for it."

Imagination Inflation

The finding that an external suggestion can lead to the construction of false childhood memories helps us understand the process by which false memories arise. It is natural to wonder whether this research is applicable in real situations such as being interrogated by law officers or in psychotherapy. Although strong suggestion may not routinely occur in police questioning or therapy, suggestion in the form of an imagination exercise sometimes does. For instance, when trying to obtain a confession, law officers may ask a suspect to imagine having participated in a criminal act. Some mental health professionals encourage patients to imagine childhood events as a way of recovering supposedly hidden memories.

Surveys of clinical psychologists reveal that 11 percent instruct their clients to "let the imagination run wild," and 22 percent tell their clients to "give free rein to the imagination." Therapist Wendy Maltz, author of a popular book on childhood sexual abuse, advocates telling the patient: "Spend time imagin-

ing that you were sexually abused, without worrying about accuracy, proving anything, or having your ideas make sense…. Ask yourself…these questions: What time of day is it? Where are you? Indoors or outdoors? What kind of things are happening? Is there one or more person with you?" Maltz further recommends that therapists continue to ask questions such as "Who would have been likely perpetrators? When were you most vulnerable to sexual abuse in your life?"

The increasing use of such imagination exercises led me and several colleagues to wonder about their consequences. What happens when people imagine childhood experiences that did not happen to them? Does imagining a childhood event increase confidence that it occurred? To explore this, we designed a three-stage procedure. We first asked individuals to indicate the likelihood that certain events happened to them during their childhood. The list contains 40 events, each rated on a scale ranging from "definitely did not happen" to "definitely did happen." Two weeks later we asked the participants to imagine that they had experienced some of these events. Different subjects were asked to imagine different events. Sometime later the participants again were asked to respond to the original list of 40 childhood events, indicating how likely it was that these events actually happened to them.

Consider one of the imagination exercises. Participants are told to imagine playing inside at home after school, hearing a strange noise outside, running toward the window, tripping, falling, reaching out and breaking the window with their hand. In addition, we asked participants questions such as "What did you trip on? How did you feel?"

In one study 24 percent of the participants who imagined the broken-window scenario later reported an increase in confidence that the event had occurred, whereas only 12 percent of those who were not asked to imagine the incident reported an increase in the likelihood that it had taken place. We found this "imagination inflation" effect in each of the eight events that participants were asked to imagine. A number of possible explanations come to mind. An obvious one is that an act of imagination simply makes the event seem more familiar and that familiarity is mistakenly related to childhood memories rather than to the act of imagination. Such source confusion—when a person does not remember the source of information—can be especially acute for the distant experiences of childhood.

Studies by Lyn Goff and Henry L. Roediger III of Washington University of recent rather than childhood experiences more directly connect imagined actions to the construction of false memory. During the initial session, the researchers instructed participants to perform the stated action, imagine doing it or just listen to the statement and do nothing else. The actions were simple ones: knock on the table, lift the stapler, break the toothpick, cross your fingers, roll your eyes. During the second session, the participants were asked to imagine some of the actions that they had not previously performed. During the final session, they answered questions about what actions they actually performed during the initial session. The investigators found that the more times participants imagined an unperformed action, the more likely they were to remember having performed it.

Impossible Memories

It is highly unlikely that an adult can recall genuine episodic memories from the first year of life, in part because the hippocampus, which plays a key role in the creation of memories, has not matured enough to form and store long-lasting memories that can be retrieved in adulthood. A procedure for planting "impossible" memories about experiences that occur shortly after birth has been developed by the late Nicholas Spanos and his collaborators at Carleton University. Individuals are led to believe that they have well-coordinated eye movements and visual exploration skills probably because they were born in hospitals that hung swinging, colored mobiles over infant cribs. To confirm whether they had such an experience, half the participants are hypnotized, age-regressed to the day after birth and asked what they remembered. The other half of the group participates in a "guided mnemonic restructuring" procedure that uses age regression as well as active encouragement to re-create the infant experiences by imagining them.

Spanos and his co-workers found that the vast majority of their subjects were susceptible to these memory-planting procedures. Both the hypnotic and guided participants reported infant memories. Surprisingly, the guided group did so somewhat more (95 versus 70 percent). Both groups remembered the colored mobile at a relatively high rate (56 percent of the guided group and 46 percent of the hypnotic subjects). Many participants who did not remember the

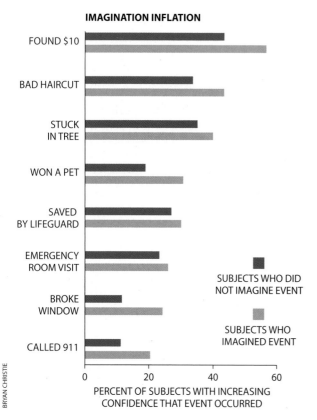

IMAGINATION INFLATION

FOUND $10
BAD HAIRCUT
STUCK IN TREE
WON A PET
SAVED BY LIFEGUARD
EMERGENCY ROOM VISIT
BROKE WINDOW
CALLED 911

■ SUBJECTS WHO DID NOT IMAGINE EVENT

■ SUBJECTS WHO IMAGINED EVENT

0   20   40   60
PERCENT OF SUBJECTS WITH INCREASING CONFIDENCE THAT EVENT OCCURRED

IMAGINING AN EVENT can increase a person's belief that the fictitious event actually happened. To study the "imagination inflation" effect, the author and her colleagues asked participants to indicate on a scale the likelihood that each of 40 events occurred during their childhood. Two weeks later they were given guidance in imagining some of the events they said had not taken place and then were asked to rate the original 40 events again. Whereas all participants showed increased confidence that the events had occurred, those who took part in actively imagining the events reported an even greater increase.

Creating False Memories

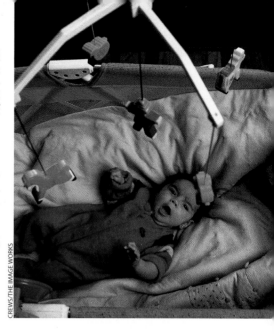

MEMORIES OF INFANCY—such as a mobile hanging over a crib—can be induced even though it is highly unlikely that events from the first year of life can be recalled. In a study by the late Nicholas Spanos and his colleagues at Carleton University, "impossible" memories of the first day of life were planted using either hypnosis or a guided mnemonic restructuring procedure. The mobile was "remembered" by 46 percent of the hypnotized group and by 56 percent of the guided group.

mobile did recall other things, such as doctors, nurses, bright lights, cribs and masks. Also, in both groups, of those who reported memories of infancy, 49 percent felt that they were real memories, as opposed to 16 percent who claimed that they were merely fantasies. These findings confirm earlier studies that many individuals can be led to construct complex, vivid and detailed false memories via a rather simple procedure. Hypnosis clearly is not necessary.

How False Memories Form

In the lost-in-the-mall study, implantation of false memory occurred when another person, usually a family member, claimed that the incident happened. Corroboration of an event by another person can be a powerful technique for instilling a false memory. In fact, merely claiming to have seen a person do something can lead that person to make a false confession of wrongdoing.

This effect was demonstrated in a study by Saul M. Kassin and his colleagues at Williams College, who investigated the reactions of individuals falsely accused of damaging a computer by pressing the wrong key. The innocent participants initially denied the charge, but when a confederate said that she had seen them perform the action, many participants signed a confession, internalized guilt for the act and went on to confabulate details that were consistent with that belief. These findings show that false

incriminating evidence can induce people to accept guilt for a crime they did not commit and even to develop memories to support their guilty feelings.

Research is beginning to give us an understanding of how false memories of complete, emotional and self-participatory experiences are created in adults. First, there are social demands on individuals to remember; for instance, researchers exert some pressure on participants in a study to come up with memories. Second, memory construction by imagining events can be explicitly encouraged when people are having trouble remembering. And, finally, individuals can be encouraged not to think about whether their constructions are real or not. Creation of false memories is most likely to occur when these external factors are present, whether in an experimental setting, in a therapeutic setting or during everyday activities.

False memories are constructed by combining actual memories with the content of suggestions received from others. During the process, individuals may forget the source of the information. This is a classic example of source confusion, in which the content and the source become dissociated.

Of course, because we can implant false childhood memories in some individuals in no way implies that all memories that arise after suggestion are necessarily false. Put another way, although experimental work on the creation of false memories may raise doubt about

the validity of long-buried memories, such as repeated trauma, it in no way disproves them. Without corroboration, there is little that can be done to help even the most experienced evaluator to differentiate true memories from ones that were suggestively planted.

The precise mechanisms by which such false memories are constructed await further research. We still have much to learn about the degree of confidence and the characteristics of false memories created in these ways, and we need to discover what types of individuals are particularly susceptible to these forms of suggestion and who is resistant.

As we continue this work, it is important to heed the cautionary tale in the data we have already obtained: mental health professionals and others must be aware of how greatly they can influence the recollection of events and of the urgent need for maintaining restraint in situations in which imagination is used as an aid in recovering presumably lost memories.   SA

The Author

ELIZABETH F. LOFTUS is professor of psychology and adjunct professor of law at the University of Washington. She received her Ph.D. in psychology from Stanford University in 1970. Her research has focused on human memory, eyewitness testimony and courtroom procedure. Loftus has published 18 books and more than 250 scientific articles and has served as an expert witness or consultant in hundreds of trials, including the McMartin preschool molestation case. Her book *Eyewitness Testimony* won a National Media Award from the American Psychological Foundation. She has received honorary doctorates from Miami University, Leiden University and John Jay College of Criminal Justice. Loftus was recently elected president of the American Psychological Society.

Further Reading

THE MYTH OF REPRESSED MEMORY. Elizabeth F. Loftus and Katherine Ketcham. St. Martin's Press, 1994.
THE SOCIAL PSYCHOLOGY OF FALSE CONFESSIONS: COMPLIANCE, INTERNALIZATION, AND CONFABULATION. Saul M. Kassin and Katherine L. Kiechel in *Psychological Science*, Vol. 7, No. 3, pages 125–128; May 1996.
IMAGINATION INFLATION: IMAGINING A CHILDHOOD EVENT INFLATES CONFIDENCE THAT IT OCCURRED. Maryanne Garry, Charles G. Manning, Elizabeth F. Loftus and Steven J. Sherman in *Psychonomic Bulletin and Review*, Vol. 3, No. 2, pages 208–214; June 1996.
REMEMBERING OUR PAST: STUDIES IN AUTOBIOGRAPHICAL MEMORY. Edited by David C. Rubin. Cambridge University Press, 1996.
SEARCHING FOR MEMORY: THE BRAIN, THE MIND, AND THE PAST. Daniel L. Schacter. BasicBooks, 1996.

Attention-Deficit Hyperactivity Disorder

A new theory suggests the disorder results from a failure in self-control.
ADHD may arise when key brain circuits do not develop
properly, perhaps because of an altered gene or genes

by Russell A. Barkley

YAN NASCIMBENE

As I watched five-year-old Keith in the waiting room of my office, I could see why his parents said he was having such a tough time in kindergarten. He hopped from chair to chair, swinging his arms and legs restlessly, and then began to fiddle with the light switches, turning the lights on and off again to everyone's annoyance—all the while talking nonstop. When his mother encouraged him to join a group of other children busy in the playroom, Keith butted into a game that was already in progress and took over, causing the other children to complain of his bossiness and drift away to other activities. Even when Keith had the toys to himself, he fidgeted aimlessly with them and seemed unable to entertain himself quietly. Once I examined him more fully, my initial suspicions were confirmed: Keith had attention-deficit hyperactivity disorder (ADHD).

Since the 1940s, psychiatrists have applied various labels to children who are hyperactive and inordinately inattentive and impulsive. Such youngsters have been considered to have "minimal brain dysfunction," "brain-injured child syndrome," "hyperkinetic reaction of childhood," "hyperactive child syndrome" and, most recently, "attention-deficit disorder." The frequent name changes reflect how uncertain researchers have been about the underlying causes of, and even the precise diagnostic criteria for, the disorder.

Within the past several years, however, those of us who study ADHD have begun to clarify its symptoms and causes and have found that it may have a genetic underpinning. Today's view of the basis of the condition is strikingly different from that of just a few years ago. We are finding that ADHD is not a disorder of attention per se, as had long been assumed. Rather it arises as a developmental failure in the brain circuitry that underlies inhibition and self-control. This loss of self-control in turn impairs other important brain functions crucial for maintaining attention, including the ability to defer immediate rewards for later, greater gain.

ADHD involves two sets of symptoms: inattention and a combination of hyper-

CHILDREN WITH ADHD cannot control their responses to their environment. This lack of control makes them hyperactive, inattentive and impulsive.

active and impulsive behaviors [*see table on next page*]. Most children are more active, distractible and impulsive than adults. And they are more inconsistent, affected by momentary events and dominated by objects in their immediate environment. The younger the children, the less able they are to be aware of time or to give priority to future events over more immediate wants. Such behaviors are signs of a problem, however, when children display them significantly more than their peers do.

Boys are at least three times as likely as girls to develop the disorder; indeed, some studies have found that boys with ADHD outnumber girls with the condition by nine to one, possibly because boys are genetically more prone to disorders of the nervous system. The behavior patterns that typify ADHD usually arise between the ages of three and five. Even so, the age of onset can vary widely: some children do not develop symptoms until late childhood or even early adolescence. Why their symptoms are delayed remains unclear.

Huge numbers of people are affected. Many studies estimate that between 2 and 9.5 percent of all school-age children worldwide have ADHD; researchers have identified it in every nation and culture they have studied. What is more, the condition, which was once thought to ease with age, can persist into adulthood. For example, roughly two thirds of 158 children with ADHD my colleagues and I evaluated in the 1970s still had the disorder in their twenties. And many of those who no longer fit the clinical description of ADHD were still having significant adjustment problems at work, in school or in other social settings.

To help children (and adults) with ADHD, psychiatrists and psychologists must better understand the causes of the disorder. Because researchers have traditionally viewed ADHD as a problem in the realm of attention, some have suggested that it stems from an inability of the brain to filter competing sensory inputs, such as sights and sounds. But recently scientists led by Joseph A. Sergeant of the University of Amsterdam have shown that children with ADHD do not have difficulty in that area; instead they cannot inhibit their impulsive motor responses to such input. Other researchers have found that children with ADHD are less capable of preparing motor responses in anticipation of

events and are insensitive to feedback about errors made in those responses. For example, in a commonly used test of reaction time, children with ADHD are less able than other children to ready themselves to press one of several keys when they see a warning light. They also do not slow down after making mistakes in such tests in order to improve their accuracy.

The Search for a Cause

No one knows the direct and immediate causes of the difficulties experienced by children with ADHD, although advances in neurological imaging techniques and genetics promise to clarify this issue over the next five years. Already they have yielded clues, albeit ones that do not yet fit together into a coherent picture.

Imaging studies over the past decade have indicated which brain regions might malfunction in patients with ADHD and thus account for the symptoms of the condition. That work suggests the involvement of the prefrontal cortex, part of the cerebellum, and at least two of the clusters of nerve cells deep in the brain that are collectively known as the basal ganglia [*see illustration on page 45*]. In a 1996 study F. Xavier Castellanos, Judith L. Rapoport and their colleagues at the National Institute of Mental Health found that the right prefrontal cortex and two basal ganglia called the caudate nucleus and the globus pallidus are significantly smaller than normal in children with ADHD. Earlier this year Castellanos's group found that the vermis region of the cerebellum is also smaller in ADHD children.

The imaging findings make sense because the brain areas that are reduced in size in children with ADHD are the very ones that regulate attention. The right prefrontal cortex, for example, is involved in "editing" one's behavior, resisting distractions and developing an awareness of self and time. The caudate nucleus and the globus pallidus help to switch off automatic responses to allow more careful deliberation by the cortex and to coordinate neurological input among various regions of the cortex. The exact role of the cerebellar vermis is unclear, but early studies suggest it may play a role in regulating motivation.

What causes these structures to shrink in the brains of those with ADHD? No one knows, but many studies have sug-

Diagnosing ADHD

Psychiatrists diagnose attention-deficit hyperactivity disorder (ADHD) if the individual displays six or more of the following symptoms of inattention or six or more symptoms of hyperactivity and impulsivity. The signs must occur often and be present for at least six months to a degree that is maladaptive and inconsistent with the person's developmental level. In addition, some of the symptoms must have caused impairment before the age of seven and must now be causing impairment in two or more settings. Some must also be leading to significant impairment in social, academic or occupational functioning; none should occur exclusively as part of another disorder. (Adapted with permission from the fourth edition of the *Diagnostic and Statistical Manual of Mental Disorders.* ©1994 American Psychiatric Association.)

INATTENTION
- Fails to give close attention to details or makes careless mistakes in schoolwork, work or other activities
- Has difficulty sustaining attention in tasks or play activities
- Does not seem to listen when spoken to directly
- Does not follow through on instructions and fails to finish schoolwork, chores or duties in the workplace
- Has difficulty organizing tasks and activities
- Avoids, dislikes or is reluctant to engage in tasks that require sustained mental effort (such as schoolwork)
- Loses things necessary for tasks or activities (such as toys, school assignments, pencils, books or tools)
- Is easily distracted by extraneous stimuli
- Is forgetful in daily activities

HYPERACTIVITY AND IMPULSIVITY
- Fidgets with hands or feet or squirms in seat
- Leaves seat in classroom or in other situations in which remaining seated is expected
- Runs about or climbs excessively in situations in which it is inappropriate (in adolescents or adults, subjective feelings of restlessness)
- Has difficulty playing or engaging in leisure activities quietly
- Is "on the go" or acts as if "driven by a motor"
- Talks excessively
- Blurts out answers before questions have been completed
- Has difficulty awaiting turns
- Interrupts or intrudes on others

LISA BURNETT

gested that mutations in several genes that are normally very active in the prefrontal cortex and basal ganglia might play a role. Most researchers now believe that ADHD is a polygenic disorder—that is, that more than one gene contributes to it.

Early tips that faulty genetics underlie ADHD came from studies of the relatives of children with the disorder. For instance, the siblings of children with ADHD are between five and seven times more likely to develop the syndrome than children from unaffected families. And the children of a parent who has ADHD have up to a 50 percent chance of experiencing the same difficulties.

The most conclusive evidence that genetics can contribute to ADHD, however, comes from studies of twins. Jacquelyn J. Gillis, then at the University of Colorado, and her colleagues reported in 1992 that the ADHD risk of a child whose identical twin has the disorder is between 11 and 18 times greater than that of a nontwin sibling of a child with ADHD; between 55 and 92 percent of the identical twins of children with ADHD eventually develop the condition.

One of the largest twin studies of ADHD was conducted by Helene Gjone and Jon M. Sundet of the University of Oslo with Jim Stevenson of the University of Southampton in England. It involved 526 identical twins, who inherit exactly the same genes, and 389 fraternal twins, who are no more alike genetically than siblings born years apart. The team found that ADHD has a heritability approaching 80 percent, meaning that up to 80 percent of the differences in attention, hyperactivity and impulsivity between people with ADHD and those without the disorder can be explained by genetic factors.

Nongenetic factors that have been linked to ADHD include premature birth, maternal alcohol and tobacco use, exposure to high levels of lead in early childhood and brain injuries—especially those that involve the prefrontal cortex. But even together, these factors can account for only between 20 and 30 percent of ADHD cases among boys; among girls, they account for an even smaller percentage. (Contrary to popular belief, neither dietary factors, such as the amount of sugar a child consumes, nor poor child-rearing methods have been consistently shown to contribute to ADHD.)

Which genes are defective? Perhaps those that dictate the way in which the brain uses dopamine, one of the chemicals known as neurotransmitters that convey messages from one nerve cell, or neuron, to another. Dopamine is secreted by neurons in specific parts of the brain to inhibit or modulate the activity of other neurons, particularly those involved in emotion and movement. The movement disorders of Parkinson's disease, for example, are caused by the death of dopamine-secreting neurons in

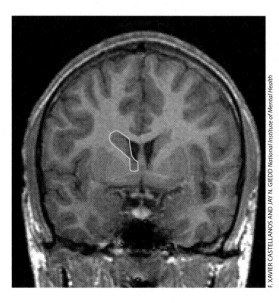

NORMAL BRAIN image outlines the right caudate nucleus (*yellow*) and the globus pallidus (*red*), brain structures that regulate attention and that are reduced in size in children with ADHD.

F. XAVIER CASTELLANOS AND JAY N. GIEDD *National Institute of Mental Health*

Attention-Deficit Hyperactivity Disorder

BRAIN STRUCTURES affected in ADHD use dopamine to communicate with one another (*green arrows*). Genetic studies suggest that people with ADHD might have alterations in genes encoding either the D4 dopamine receptor, which receives incoming signals, or the dopamine transporter, which scavenges released dopamine for reuse. The substantia nigra, where the death of dopamine-producing neurons causes Parkinson's disease, is not affected in ADHD.

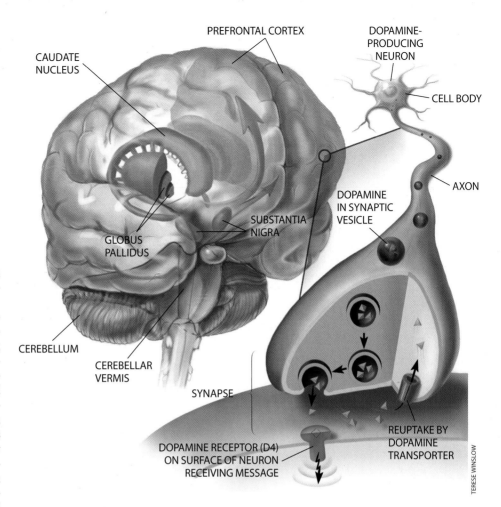

PREFRONTAL CORTEX

DOPAMINE-PRODUCING NEURON

CAUDATE NUCLEUS

CELL BODY

AXON

DOPAMINE IN SYNAPTIC VESICLE

SUBSTANTIA NIGRA

GLOBUS PALLIDUS

CEREBELLUM

CEREBELLAR VERMIS

SYNAPSE

REUPTAKE BY DOPAMINE TRANSPORTER

DOPAMINE RECEPTOR (D4) ON SURFACE OF NEURON RECEIVING MESSAGE

TERESE WINSLOW

a region of the brain underneath the basal ganglia called the substantia nigra.

Some impressive studies specifically implicate genes that encode, or serve as the blueprint for, dopamine receptors and transporters; these genes are very active in the prefrontal cortex and basal ganglia. Dopamine receptors sit on the surface of certain neurons. Dopamine delivers its message to those neurons by binding to the receptors. Dopamine transporters protrude from neurons that secrete the neurotransmitter; they take up unused dopamine so that it can be used again. Mutations in the dopamine receptor gene can render receptors less sensitive to dopamine. Conversely, mutations in the dopamine transporter gene can yield overly effective transporters that scavenge secreted dopamine before it has a chance to bind to dopamine receptors on a neighboring neuron.

In 1995 Edwin H. Cook and his colleagues at the University of Chicago reported that children with ADHD were more likely than others to have a particular variation in the dopamine transporter gene *DAT1*. Similarly, in 1996 Gerald J. LaHoste of the University of California at Irvine and his co-workers found that a variant of the dopamine receptor gene *D4* is more common among children with ADHD. But each of these studies involved 40 or 50 children—a relatively small number—so their findings are now being confirmed in larger studies.

From Genes to Behavior

How do the brain-structure and genetic defects observed in children with ADHD lead to the characteristic behaviors of the disorder? Ultimately,

they might be found to underlie impaired behavioral inhibition and self-control, which I have concluded are the central deficits in ADHD.

Self-control—or the capacity to inhibit or delay one's initial motor (and perhaps emotional) responses to an event—is a critical foundation for the performance of any task. As most children grow up, they gain the ability to engage in mental activities, known as executive functions, that help them deflect distractions, recall goals and take the steps needed to reach them. To achieve a goal in work or play, for instance, people need to be able to remember their aim (use hindsight), prompt themselves about what they need to do to reach that goal (use forethought), keep their emotions reined in and motivate themselves. Unless a person can inhibit interfering thoughts and impulses, none of these functions can be carried out successfully.

In the early years, the executive functions are performed externally: children might talk out loud to themselves while remembering a task or puzzling out a problem. As children mature, they internalize, or make private, such executive functions, which prevents others from knowing their thoughts. Children with

ADHD, in contrast, seem to lack the restraint needed to inhibit the public performance of these executive functions.

The executive functions can be grouped into four mental activities. One is the operation of working memory—holding information in the mind while working on a task, even if the original stimulus that provided the information is gone. Such remembering is crucial to timeliness and goal-directed behavior: it provides the means for hindsight, forethought, preparation and the ability to imitate the complex, novel behavior of others—all of which are impaired in people with ADHD.

The internalization of self-directed speech is another executive function. Before the age of six, most children speak out loud to themselves frequently, reminding themselves how to perform a particular task or trying to cope with a problem, for example. ("Where did I put that book? Oh, I left it under the desk.") In elementary school, such private speech evolves into inaudible muttering; it usually disappears by age 10 [see "Why Children Talk to Themselves," by Laura E. Berk; SCIENTIFIC AMERICAN, November 1994]. Internalized, self-directed speech allows one to

A Psychological Model of ADHD

A loss of behavioral inhibition and self-control leads to the following disruptions in brain functioning:

IMPAIRED FUNCTION	CONSEQUENCE	EXAMPLE
Nonverbal working memory	Diminished sense of time Inability to hold events in mind Defective hindsight Defective forethought	Nine-year-old Jeff routinely forgets important responsibilities, such as deadlines for book reports or an after-school appointment with the principal
Internalization of self-directed speech	Deficient rule-governed behavior Poor self-guidance and self-questioning	Five-year-old Audrey talks too much and cannot give herself useful directions silently on how to perform a task
Self-regulation of mood, motivation and level of arousal	Displays all emotions publicly; cannot censor them Diminished self-regulation of drive and motivation	Eight-year-old Adam cannot maintain the persistent effort required to read a story appropriate for his age level and is quick to display his anger when frustrated by assigned schoolwork
Reconstitution (ability to break down observed behaviors into component parts that can be recombined into new behaviors in pursuit of a goal)	Limited ability to analyze behaviors and synthesize new behaviors Inability to solve problems	Fourteen-year-old Ben stops doing a homework assignment when he realizes that he has only two of the five assigned questions; he does not think of a way to solve the problem, such as calling a friend to get the other three questions

LISA BURNETT

reflect to oneself, to follow rules and instructions, to use self-questioning as a form of problem solving and to construct "meta-rules," the basis for understanding the rules for using rules—all quickly and without tipping one's hand to others. Laura E. Berk and her colleagues at Illinois State University reported in 1991 that the internalization of self-directed speech is delayed in boys with ADHD.

A third executive mental function consists of controlling emotions, motivation and state of arousal. Such control helps individuals achieve goals by enabling them to delay or alter potentially distracting emotional reactions to a particular event and to generate private emotions and motivation. Those who rein in their immediate passions can also behave in more socially acceptable ways.

The final executive function, reconstitution, actually encompasses two separate processes: breaking down observed behaviors and combining the parts into new actions not previously learned from experience. The capacity for reconstitution gives humans a great degree of fluency, flexibility and creativity; it allows individuals to propel themselves toward a goal without having to learn all the needed steps by rote. It permits children as they mature to direct their behavior

across increasingly longer intervals by combining behaviors into ever longer chains to attain a goal. Initial studies imply that children with ADHD are less capable of reconstitution than are other children.

I suggest that like self-directed speech, the other three executive functions become internalized during typical neural development in early childhood. Such privatization is essential for creating visual imagery and verbal thought. As children grow up, they develop the capacity to behave covertly, to mask some of their behaviors or feelings from others. Perhaps because of faulty genetics or embryonic development, children with ADHD have not attained this ability and therefore display too much public behavior and speech. It is my assertion that the inattention, hyperactivity and impulsivity of children with ADHD are caused by their failure to be guided by internal instructions and by their inability to curb their own inappropriate behaviors.

Prescribing Self-Control

If, as I have outlined, ADHD is a failure of behavioral inhibition that delays the ability to privatize and execute the four executive mental functions I

have described, the finding supports the theory that children with ADHD might be helped by a more structured environment. Greater structure can be an important complement to any drug therapy the children might receive. Currently children (and adults) with ADHD often receive drugs such as Ritalin that boost their capacity to inhibit and regulate impulsive behaviors. These drugs act by inhibiting the dopamine transporter, increasing the time that dopamine has to bind to its receptors on other neurons.

Such compounds (which, despite their inhibitory effects, are known as psychostimulants) have been found to improve the behavior of between 70 and 90 percent of children with ADHD older than five years. Children with ADHD who take such medication not only are less impulsive, restless and distractible but are also better able to hold important information in mind, to be more productive academically, and to have more internalized speech and better self-control. As a result, they tend to be liked better by other children and to experience less punishment for their actions, which improves their self-image.

My model suggests that in addition to psychostimulants—and perhaps antidepressants, for some children—treat-

Attention-Deficit Hyperactivity Disorder

PSYCHOLOGICAL TESTS used in ADHD research include the four depicted here. The tower-building test (*upper left*), in which the subject is asked to assemble balls into a tower to mimic an illustration, measures forethought, planning and persistence. The math test (*upper right*) assesses working memory and problem-solving ability. In the auditory attention test (*below*), the subject must select the appropriate colored tile according to taped instructions, despite distracting words. The time estimation test (*lower right*) measures visual attention and subjective sense of time intervals. The subject is asked to hold down a key to illuminate a lightbulb on a computer screen for the same length of time that another bulb was illuminated previously.

PHOTOGRAPHS BY STEPHEN ROSE *Gamma Liaison*

ment for ADHD should include training parents and teachers in specific and more effective methods for managing the behavioral problems of children with the disorder. Such methods involve making the consequences of a child's actions more frequent and immediate and increasing the external use of prompts and cues about rules and time intervals. Parents and teachers must aid children with ADHD by anticipating events for them, breaking future tasks down into smaller and more immediate steps, and using artificial immediate rewards. All these steps serve to externalize time, rules and consequences as a replacement for the weak internal forms of information, rules and motivation of children with ADHD.

In some instances, the problems of ADHD children may be severe enough to warrant their placement in special education programs. Although such programs are not intended as a cure for the child's difficulties, they typically do provide a smaller, less competitive and more supportive environment in which the child can receive individual instruction. The hope is that once children learn techniques to overcome their deficits in self-control, they will be able to function outside such programs.

There is no cure for ADHD, but much more is now known about effectively coping with and managing this persistent and troubling developmental disorder. The day is not far off when genetic testing for ADHD may become available and more specialized medications may be designed to counter the specific genetic deficits of the children who suffer from it. **SA**

The Author

RUSSELL A. BARKLEY is director of psychology and professor of psychiatry and neurology at the University of Massachusetts Medical Center in Worcester. He received his B.A. from the University of North Carolina at Chapel Hill and his M.A. and Ph.D. from Bowling Green State University. He has studied ADHD for nearly 25 years and has written many scientific papers, book chapters and books on the subject, including *ADHD and the Nature of Self-Control* (Guilford Press, 1997) and *Attention-Deficit Hyperactivity Disorder: A Handbook for Diagnosis and Treatment* (Guilford Press, 1998).

Further Reading

THE EPIDEMIOLOGY OF ATTENTION-DEFICIT HYPERACTIVITY DISORDER. Peter Szatmari in *Child and Adolescent Psychiatric Clinics of North America*, Vol. 1. Edited by G. Weiss. W. B. Saunders, 1992.
HYPERACTIVE CHILDREN GROWN UP. Gabrielle Weiss and Lily Trokenberg Hechtman. Guilford Press, 1993.
TAKING CHARGE OF ADHD: THE COMPLETE, AUTHORITATIVE GUIDE FOR PARENTS. R. A. Barkley. Guilford Press, 1995.
DOPAMINE *D4* RECEPTOR GENE POLYMORPHISM IS ASSOCIATED WITH ATTENTION DEFICIT HYPERACTIVITY DISORDER. G. J. LaHoste et al. in *Molecular Psychiatry*, Vol. 1, No. 2, pages 121–124; May 1996.

This Psychology supplement is the product of a partnership between Worth Publishers and Scientific American, publishers of the nation's leading science magazine.

www.worthpublishers.com
www.sciam.com

Worth Publishers
41 Madison Avenue
New York, NY 10010

ISBN 0-7167-5319-7

90000

EAN

9 780716 753193